BACKYARD BBQ

The Art of Smokology!®

"Where Backyard Spice Meets Life"™

Richard W. McPeake
(Sultan of Smoke)
Educator of "Que"
Rib Star® Award Winning BBQ

BACKYARD BBQ

The Art of Smokology!®

"Where Backyard Spice Meets Life"™

Richard W. McPeake
Educator of "Que"
Rib Stars® Award Winning BBQ

Book Cover designed by John Thomsen
of TASTEFUL IDEAS.

Printed in the United States of America.
ISBN: 0-9718014-2-8
ISBN-13: 978-0-9718014-2-4

CONTENTS

RECIPES

ACKNOWLEDGMENTS

I want to thank my wonderful wife Kris, who allows me to use a lot of my weekends, teaching and competing, and who never complains about my love for this hobby. Also to my kids, Jessica and Jonathan, who are the two best kids a father could ask for and who helped perfect the BBQ sauces.

To my GREAT friends:

Jim & Joan Cattey, for their words of wisdom and their friendship. They also allow me to just hang out and cook things at their awesome BBQ Store, Smoke N' Fire!

Laura O'Rourke, who has given me the chance to rekindle a new spirit for my love of teaching people and allowing me the opportunity to teach.

Bruce Campbell, for his assistance in teaching classes and sharing his own love for the Art of Smoking.

Harold Colston & Hot Meat Smokers, you have become GREAT friends and bring out the best in a contest!

Phil & Linda Hopkins (Smokin' Guns BBQ), for the many discussions we have had about BBQ and for the special dinners we enjoy at contests!

There have been numerous friends, who have volunteered their time and taste buds to the many recipes that are entered in this book. Their opinions and comments have always been greatly appreciated.

I also want to acknowledge all those people who compete every weekend and every year. You are the true BBQ'ers of the world, and like me, I know that it is always a winning recipe you create for yourself. And if you happen to win a ribbon or a trophy, now and then, that's great! But we all go home winners every time, because we are doing what we love with friends!

INTRODUCTION

My decision to write Backyard BBQ, The Art of Smokology® was to update the information written in my first smoking cook-book, based on new techniques, leading to a better smoking experience. This book features new chapters like Secrets to Smoking Seafood, Brining Poultry, Proper Smoking Techniques, Tips on Smoking Meats and many new recipes.

Teaching smokology classes has allowed me to test and demon-strate many new techniques. My experiences have made me a better chef in understanding what the beginner smoker wants to learn. To date I have taught over 150 classes teaching over 4000 people in The Art of Smokology® and Grilling.

This book is intended to help the beginner become a successful smoker and the competitor to increase their choices of recipes from which to learn.

And remember, backyard bbq is "Where Backyard Spice Meets Life"

Enjoy! It's Backyard Smoking time!

Chef Richard McPeake
"Sultan of Smoke"
Educator of "Que"

These new techniques are being taught in my Smoking & BBQ classes at The Culinary Center of Kansas City in Overland Park, Kansas, in conjunction with the Midwest Barbecue Institute ("MBQI"). The Culinary Center features several different classes on the Art of Smokology.

THE CULINARY CENTER of KANSAS CITY

www.kcculinary.com
cook@kcculinary.com

SULTAN'S STARTING FACTS

SMOKERS:

There are several types of smokers that can be used for smoking. Each person will have their own belief of which one to use. I believe that you should look at as many different ones as possible. Go to several contests and see what people are using, and remember that bigger is not better. In 1982, I was on a Grand Champion team and we used Weber Kettles and Brinkmans! Now I only use the Good-One smoker.

Dry Smokers:

These smoker are in horizontal & vertical styles, using two different chambers; one on the side for the fire and the main chamber for meats. These can also have a water pan added to them, but will not create the same moisture as an upright wet smoker. The natural juices produced by the meat are enough moisture for the smoker. Dry smokers will tend to run higher than wet smokers. They are also easier to maintain temperatures for longer periods of time, since they have side and top vents for controlling the air flow and the amount of smoke captured in the meat chamber. These vents also help control the amount of smoke you want to penetrate your product. There are many different types and brands of horizontal smokers. I found that the internet is a great starting point.

Wet Smokers:

Most of these smokers are of the upright versions. They have a tier method of cooking with a coal pan on the bottom, a water pan, and then usually two or three racks above the water pan. The water pan produces water vapors as the water heats above the fire source. Water smokers are commonly used when shorter periods of smoking time is required and for thinner cuts of meats. Most water smokers will be harder to raise to the 225° mark because of the water vapors in the internal smoker. These smokers are ideal for items that require less heat and shorter cooking times.

USING GRILLS FOR SMOKING:

Gas Grills:

If you are an owner of a gas grill, you can still become a backyard smoker. Gas grills lend themselves well to smoking if you take the necessary steps to smoke properly. If your gas grill is big enough and has a high cover and a dual fire system, the easiest way to smoke is to light one half of your grill and place a metal wood chip holder, with the desired wood chips, over the fire side. On the side that is not lit, place the meat to be smoked directly on the grill grates. You may also add a small water pan below the grate, if there is room or just set a small deep pan on the grill between the wood box and meat. Once the desired temperature of 210-225° is reached, use the heat control to maintain the temperature. If you do not have a wood box, you can easily make a wood chip holder by double layering aluminum foil and piercing it with several small holes to allow the heat to reach the wood and produce small quantities of wood flavor.

Weber Kettle Grills:

Weber grills make great smokers for the beginner. They have a huge body and allow you plenty of room to build off set fires with added wood. They also allow you to do indirect heat, which helps for producing a better smoked product. Indirect cooking in a Weber is easy because it allows you several choices. You can do an off set fire, placing the fire to one side and the cooked product to the other, with a water pan underneath it. Or, you can do a dual off set fire with the water pan in the middle and the product placed in the middle of the grill, directly over the water pan.

TYPES OF FUEL:

Many BBQ'ers have their own personal preferences about what to use for the main fuel in their smoker or grill. I have worked personally and professionally with many different types.

Charcoal Choices:

There are three types of "charcoal".

1) The first and best choice is Natural Chunk or Lump charcoal, that is from 100% wood and has been pyrolyzed or turned from hard wood into charcoal. This fuel will burn 2.5 to 3 times hotter than a briquette and has less ash and a dramatically cleaner flavor.

2) The second best option is Natural Briquettes. These are compressed lump coal fines that have similar performance as chunk with slightly less heat and a bit more ash.

3) The last alternative is what 20th century marketing has deluded most people into thinking "charcoal" really is. The "K" product and its various generic clones are only 20-30% natural wood charcoal. The rest is made up of bituminous coal dust, coke (the condensate from petroleum refineries), starch, mineral binders and a splash of good old petroleum to make it all burn again! Tasty, hey? No wonder so many people get indigestion when they eat BBQ even though it has nothing to do with the meat or the rub!!!

Wood:

There are unlimited flavors of wood available, and flavor is what you want. Wood should be use to enhance your product and give the added taste that you are seeking. I prefer to start with coal and use the wood for the beginning flavor to the product. Using wood throughout the whole cooking process can lead to a harsh flavor, especially if the smoking chamber has a small air space ratio to meat density. Also when using wood, try to remove as much excess bark as possible, since this can also lead to a harsh flavor in your meats.

Fruit woods and assorted special woods lend themselves well to add an additional dimension to your finished product. The use of these different woods depends on your product, sweetness level, mops, rubs and finishing sauce. The best method for this determination is trial and error. Find out what you like best. Try different woods each time to see the difference in flavor for each dish.

Types of Woods:
The traditional woods for smoking are HICKORY and OAK. Here are some woods suitable for smoking:

ALMOND - A sweet smoke flavor. Good with all meats.

APPLE - Very mild fruity flavor, slightly sweet. Good with poultry and pork.

CHERRY - Mild and fruity. Good with poultry, pork and beef.

SUGAR MAPLE - One of my favorites! This wood adds a nice sweet favor and burns very clean. Great on pork butts, spare ribs and chicken.

GRAPEVINES - Produces a lot of smoke. Rich and fruity with a slight tart flavor. Good with poultry, red meats, game and lamb.

HICKORY - Most commonly used wood for smoking--the strong, heavy bacon flavor. Good with pork, ham and beef.

MAPLE - Smoky, mellow and slightly sweet. Good with pork, poultry and small game birds.

MESQUITE - Strong earthy flavor. Good with beef, fish, chicken, and game. One of the hottest burning woods!

OAK - Nice heavy smoke flavor. WHITE OAK makes the best coals for longer burning. Good with red meat, pork, fish and heavy game.

PEAR - A nice subtle smoke flavor. Excellent with chicken and pork.

PECAN - Sweet and mild with a flavor similar to hickory. Good with poultry, beef and pork. Pecan is an all-around good smoking wood. (Another one of my favorites for Pork.)

SWEET FRUIT WOODS - APRICOT, PLUM, PEACH, NECTARINE - Great on most white or pink meats, including chicken, turkey, pork, shrimp and lobster tails.

WALNUT - ENGLISH and BLACK - Heavy smoke flavor, needs to be mixed with lighter woods. Can be very bitter if used alone. Good with red meats and game.

Herbs & Vines:
Dried herb branches lend themselves very well to the smoking process of meats. Rosemary branches, thyme and basil branches are all excellent. Dried grape vines are an excellent source for adding additional flavor to meats, use red grape vines on meats and white grape vines on seafood.

Wood Smoke and Meat Combinations:

Wood Species	Beef	Lamb	Pork	Poultry	Seafood
Alder	X	X	X	X	X
Apple	X	X	X	X	X
Cherry		X	X	X	X
Grape		X	X	X	X
Hedge			X	X	X
Hickory		X	X	X	X
Maple			X	X	X
Mesquite	X	X	X	X	X
Mulberry	X	X	X	X	X
Oak	X	X	X	X	X
Orange			X	X	X
Peach			X	X	X
Pecan		X	X	X	X
Persimmon		X	X	X	X
Sassafras	X	X	X	X	
Walnut		X	X		

SMOKING TERMS

BBQ Bark:
The outer crust that is formed from the dry rub and smoking process on the surface of the product. The caramelizing of the rub in the first two hours gives the art of smoking its flavor. This is why it is so important to use a balanced rub to compliment the product being smoked. Most judges will look for the outer bark as a sign of a well smoked product, along with the smoke ring produced just below the bark.

Brines:
This method is done mostly with poultry and fish and uses larger amounts of salt, providing additional preservation. Most brines are made by infusing flavors with the water and salt. This penetrates the product and allows the product to absorb and retain moisture during the cooking process.

Curing:
All curing is done in the dry method using larger amounts of salt. Curing is also done to help preserve the product. The dry cure is usually added with the product for longer periods of time than a standard dry rub.

Dry Rub:
This is the dry seasoning used to flavor the meat on the outside during the smoking process. Most rubs start with equal parts of salt and sugar, then chili powder, paprika, different peppers, herb flavors, and flavoring spices.

Drafting:
This is the proper use of your vents to produce good air flow, which helps maintain your fire and temperature. Adjusting side and top vents will lower or raise your temperatures.

Jerky:
Jerky is not the same as Jerk Cooking which originated in Jamaica. Jerky cooking in America is actually the curing of the meat and smoking to preserve the product itself. It was used in the settler days to preserve meats for long journeys. My jerky's are done both

with dry rubs and some wet marinades overnight. All are done in the smokers. Meat used to make jerky should be the leanest available and have all the outer fat removed.

Marinades:

Marinades are a method of liquid flavoring for three main reasons; to tenderize the product, add flavor to the product and to add moisture to all types of meats, including seafood and poultry. Most marinades are water based, and mixed with vinegar and wine, then flavored with onion, assorted peppers and spices. Marinating differs from brining, because brining is done with larger amounts of salt to help the product retain moisture during the cooking process. Marinating is used to infuse the product with a specific flavor and to make a product tender.

Mops & Sops:

These are not interchangeable words. Mops come from the true sense of the word, using a small handled cloth mop as a basting tool. Hence, to mop. Sopping on the other hand, refers to the method of sopping the product in a liquid, during eating.

Mop tools are the cloth ended small mop, some are brush style and some are made of foam rubber. The cloth ended mop is the best tool to use. The most common tool for liquid fruit juice based mops are spray bottles, since they place an even layer of fine mist over your product. Be advised that to use a spray bottle the liquid needs to be strained of any particles (peppers, spices, leaves) and can not be thicker than the consistency of a fruit juice. Since mops are basting sauces used to add moisture during the cooking process, they should be applied **after** the first two hours of smoking, to allow the "bark" to form. Sops are flavored liquids or light thin sauces for dipping and "sopping" the product when eating.

Smoke Ring:

Smoke rings are produced by a chemical reaction between the protein, fire and moisture of the product being smoked. This ring will appear in meats cooked with woods or without woods! It is a pink color that extends from the outside surface into the meat.

The thickness of the smoke ring depends on several factors. (See Proper Smoking Techniques page 18)

True Temperature:

This is one of the most important terms. Always make sure that you know the temperature at the rack level of the product. An outside thermometer at the top part of your smoker shows you the temperature at the top layer of the smoker. The product in the middle of the smoker, being 6-9" from the top or bottom, could be as much as 50° lower. For this reason, I recommend using another oven thermometer at the same level as your product. Once you become familiar with your smoker, you will learn what the outside reading needs to be to maintain the proper or "true" temperature!

Water Pan:

A water pan can be a built in item or just a disposable pan and are used in most upright smokers. Water pans are used to produce a higher humidity level in the smoker, which is key in producing a good smoke ring.

PROPER SMOKING TECHNIQUES

Developing a Proper Smoke Ring:

This is one of the easiest but most misunderstood and mistaught process of smoking. The key to a GREAT smoke ring is understanding two components.

I.) Understand that meat protein starts to set or cook at 120° F internal temperature.

Once the protein sets, it can not and will not absorb any more smoke flavor, especially the leaner meats. Protein is completely cooked once it reaches an internal temperature of 140° F. Knowing this you will want to get your meat into the smoker as cool as possible, but not frozen. The cooler the meat, thegreater the range of temperature you have to develope your smoke ring. Example: Putting your Brisket in a smoker at 40 degrees now gives you a range of 80 degrees to develope your ring. If you put your brisket in at 60 degrees, you have now decreased your chance to develope a deeper smoke ring by 20 degrees of cooking time.

2.) Humidity and nitrates play a BIG part in developing a smoke ring.

Nitrates are produce from the wood ash being carried by the smoke, which then reacts with the myoglobin. (Oxygen carrying protein in the meat tissue). The higher the humidity is, the better your chances are to develope a deep smoke ring in your meat.

So, if you want a deeper smoke ring, get your product in your smoker at a cooler temperature. I like to keep my meat very cold, and then bring the meat out about 1 hour before smoking to allow the outside meat fibers to relax. This also helps the outer edge to absorb the smoke flavor a little faster. Start your heavier density meats (brisket and pork butts) at a lower temperature, allowing the meat to reach the 120-140 degree plateau at a slower rate. Keep the humidity level higher and you should have a nice smoke ring.

Developing a Bark:
The "bark" as it is known in the BBQ world is the outer crust developed by the rub which you use, absorbing the juices as it cooks and adheres to the meat. It is important to remember not to "mop" your smoking product to soon, since this will wash away your dry rub and you will not develope the bark. My rule of thumb is to not mop for the first two hours, allowing my dry rub to develope the bark before I will even start to mop my products.

I do not follow this rule for chicken, because chicken does not take as long to smoke and you really do not want a bark on your smoked chicken products. Plus, dry rubs should be used sparingly on any chicken products.

Applying Dry Rubs:
Dry rubs can be applied the night before, an hour before or 5 minutes before, this is really your preference. The main factor in making your decision will depend on how much salt is in the rub itself. Salt draws out important juices from your protein product. The loss of moisture will result in the product being drier. I like to put my rubs on differently for each product.

Following is when I like to put the rub on my products before placing them in the smoker.

- Pork Ribs (2 hours)
- Chicken (5 minutes before)
- Brisket (4 hours)
- Pork Butt (12 hours ahead).

If your dry rub is coming out pasty tasting or thick and wet, odds are they have to much paprika and chili powder in them, since they tend to draw extra moisture out of the product. Know your product well and then experiment with your rubs to see when it is best to apply them. As I said earlier, longer is not always better!

Mopping:

Begin your mopping after the first 2 hours of smoking. Mopping can be done by using a cloth mop, brush or spray bottles. Mopping with flavored liquids will enhance the outer flavor of the meat and compliment your dry rub. Spray bottles work well for misting your product, but the mop needs to be thin enough and strained of any particles to keep the spray head from clogging up. Use fruit juices for ribs, pork and chicken, and beef broth for brisket and beef ribs.

BUILDING A FIRE

There are several ways to start a fire, including newspaper,coal chimney, lighter fluid, wood wedges, soaked starter wood and electric coal starters. The first thing to remember is that all fires need to be started at least 20 minutes to an hour before smoking time to allow proper burning and to obtain a proper cooking temperature for smoking. A starter gel is also available which works very well and does not produce the after taste that lighter fluids do. I highly recommend this product for starting your fire. In all cases, allowing the fire to burn well will produce the best results. I recommend to avoid using lighter fluid because if you know how to build and start a proper fire, you will not need it!

Proper Lighting of Fire:

Again, the first rule in building a fire is never use lighter fluid! This will give your smoked meats an off flavor and there is no need to use it to build a proper fire. There are starter gels available that are acceptable to use.

First, start with a fire starter (chimney) bought or homemade. Make sure you have a layer of raw lump coal in your fire box. Using a little starter gel, place some of the gel in the center of the coal and create a 4" trail away from the center, which will act as a fuse for lighting. Place the starter chimney in the fire box on top of the center coals where you placed the starter gel. Fill the chimney to the top with your raw lump coal and put a little more gel on top on the coal. Light the top gel first, let burn about two minutes, then light the gel fuse. Let the coal burn until 3/4 of it is white and hot. Then, dump the hot coals into the firebox on top of the raw coals. Add another container size (fire chimney) of raw coal on top of the hot coals. Allow this to start to burn.

Homemade version : Take an empty large coffee can and punch 5 to 6 holes in the unopened bottom (using a large church key) along the side of the can just above the rim. Once you cut the holes, remove the bottom lid. Bend out the prongs from the punched holes. These prongs will hold your crumpled up newspaper. If using a starter gel, newspaper is not needed.

Leave your firebox open until the coals are burning well. Add wood and allow the fire to start to burn the wood well before shutting the fire box lid. Once you shut the firebox lid, open the side and top vents full, until the smoker preheats to 300 degrees. Once at 300 degrees, load your meat into the smoking chamber and close the door. Allow the temperature to come back to the desired smoking temperature that you want to smoke at. Adjust the vents to maintain this temperature.

I prefer to use 100% lump coal or mesquite coal. I never use briquettes in my smokers, because they burn slower, colder and tend to smoulder. Lump coal is compress wood and burns hotter and faster. You will use more, but you will be able to maintain your heat better, produce a better air flow and produce less ash.

MEATS FOR SMOKING

Beef:

There is no rule to what you can smoke, but for the most part, the two most common beef products used in smoking are brisket and beef ribs. The best rule to remember about beef is that it does not do well with too much smoke. Brisket and beef products will become very harsh when smoked with too much wood. It is best to smoke about 2 hours with wood to achieve your nice smoke ring and flavor. Then, back off the wood and go to lump coal or burnt down wood for the rest of the cooking fuel until finished. The following products are the ones I have had the most success with smoking in my smokers.

Brisket- longer cooking time required to achieve tenderness. Nothing can beat a perfect smoked brisket for a excellent backyard BBQ! The brisket can be bought whole or in separate muscles known as the *point* (the top fiberous muscle) and the *flat* (the bottom leaner muscle of the brisket.

Beef Ribs- Great to change the pace of pork ribs. Beef ribs are actually one of my favorites.

Whole Tenderloin- Outstanding and does not take as long to achieve a finished product. Already a tender meat, so cook just until you have a beautiful smoke ring and flavor.

Prime Rib - A little more tricky to cook in order to achieve an outstanding product. I prefer to smoke without the bone to get a complete smoked flavor all around.

Pork:

Pork is the best for smoking. You cannot over smoke a pork should or butt product from a flavor standpoint. Pork shoulders and butts can take a lot of smoke without the harsh flavor of the wood, unlike its counterpart beef! Pork butts are outstanding to smoke are one of the best self basting products out there. I smoke my pork butts for 8-12 hours to achieve one of the finest shredded pork products around. Plus pork takes well to numerous different rubs, mops and sauces!

Great pork products to use:

Ribs - There are three main types of ribs, all being of personal taste and texture of each individual person.

Spareribs- Larger and meatier of all the ribs, this is the King of ribs. Tends to have more fat, but because of this are more flavorful. Costs less per pound than baby back ribs.

St. Louis Ribs- These are really spareribs that have been specially trimmed, removing the excess skirt meat and cut across the sternum and cartilage. They are smaller and lighter in weight than the Spareribs.

Baby Backs- Many people prefer the baby back ribs, because they are easier to cook, tend to be more tender and are less fatty. Because of their smaller size, baby back ribs cook faster than spareribs. For these reasons, baby backs are a good rib to start with as a beginner.

Pork Butt, Picnics orShoulders - Butts come from an area above the shoulder and have the blade bone in them. Picnics, come from the leg area and have the shank bone in it. I prefer pork butts, bone in, especially since they have several muscles and a good amount of fat for self basting.

Pork Loins - They are leaner than the other above pork products, so special care is needed not to over smoke. But they are outstanding when smoked! Boneless pork loins are best for smoking.

Pork Tenderloin - Treat like beef tenderloin. They are already tender, so get your smoke flavor achieved and then make sure you don't over smoke.

Poultry & Seafood:

I love to smoke bone-in chicken breast or a boneless turkey breast for a little BBQ mopping. I recommend brining your poultry products before smoking. This will help the product to retain moisture during the cooking process. (See Brining Poultry page 43)

Chicken Breast- Brining the chicken breast before smoking, you will be able to add many different flavors and moisture. One of the most important things to be careful of when brining is to watch the amount of salt you use. Excess salt will make your chicken tough and chewy.

Whole Turkeys- Whole bone-in turkeys are great to smoke. There is nothing like a smoked turkey during the holiday season. I like to brine my turkeys for 24 hours and then also inject them with the brine before smoking.

Turkey Breast- I found the best breast to smoke is the 10-12 pound bone in breast. Marinated or brined, they are excellent for use in your smoker. And of course they smoke cook much faster than the whole turkey.

Turkey Chops- These are crosscut section chops, with the bone-in. Your butcher can cut them for you but they are easy to cut yourself. Just split the bone-in breast and cut chops across the grain. They are great for smoking or grilling.

Nothing beats smoking your own fresh seafood. Always make sure you start with the freshest product as possible. All fish should be done in a brining solution and air dried before smoking. (See Secrets to Smoking Seafood page 47)

Fish Fillets- Most fillets (salmon, trout, catfish, etc.) prepared for smoking are done in a brining liquid. Most of these liquids contain salt and some form of sugar. Try using different seasonings before you smoke the fillets (i.e. lemon pepper, blackened fine herbs, etc.) These will all enhance the final flavor of your fish.

Scallops- Smoked scallops are outstanding! They have a sweet flavor, that intensifies with smoking. Since they do not need a long smoking time, the larger scallops are better to use and are harder to over smoke.

Shrimp- The use of larger shrimp will aid in not over smoking this product. I recommend nothing smaller than a 21/25 count (shrimp per pound). I like using more of a mustard brine for shrimp before smoking. Shrimp need to be peeled before brining, marinating or smoking. When marinating shrimp for smoking, make sure you watch the amount of acid you use, since acid will set (cook) the protein in the shrimp and make them tough.

Lobster Tails- One of my favorite things to smoke is a lobster tail. First, make sure you use a **cold** water lobster tail, the meat is firmer and sweeter than warm water tails. You will pay more for cold water tails (they range from $21.95 to $27.95 per pound), but they are well worth it. I like to use a light brining solution to infuse the tail meat with some addition flavor. Remove the tails from the shell before brining, marinating or smoking. You will also need to make about 3 incisions on the bottom of the lobster tail, to keep them from curling up too much while they are smoking.

TIPS ON SELECTING MEATS

In this chapter I will mostly concentrate on the meats that are most commonly used in basic smoking. Remember, once you know what you are doing, any kind of meat can be smoked!

Briskets:

Select fresh brisket and look for briskets that are not too small! I like them if they are whole briskets (2 muscles) and no more than 12-15 pounds. A brisket is made up of two separate muscles. The top muscle is called the "point" and has several different grains running through it, making it harder to slice and is more fiberous. The bottom muscle or the "flat" is leaner and more uniform for smoking purposes.

Holding the middle of the brisket in your hand, the ends of the brisket should give a little bend down. If the brisket stays rigid, it is from an older and tougher animal. Always select the ones that give a bit, because these will cook more tender! Don't worry about the fat cover, because you can trim this yourself before cooking. Trim the excessive fat from the meat, to allow the smoke and dry rub to penetrate the meat. I recommend trimming the fat down to about 1/4" thickness.

Spareribs:

Spareribs will weight about 2-4 pounds. Always select the lighter weight ribs. These come from a smaller and usually younger animal and will be more tender, allowing for a faster cooking period. I prefer the ribs to have the sternum, cartilage and skirt meat attached. I like to remove these myself, for the simple fact that I smoke these products to be added to my baked beans.

St. Louis Style Spareribs:

These are a special trimmed Spareribs and can be just as good as baby backs when cooked right. They tend to be lighter in weight than spares, weighing about 1 3/4 - 2 pounds. Again, I prefer the smaller sized ribs. All St. Louis style ribs are free of sternum, cartilage and skirt meat.

Baby Back Ribs:

Some will argue the these are the cadillac of the rib family. Although I love baby back ribs, I do like to switch between baby backs and spareribs. I tend to think that spareribs have more flavor. For the beginner smoker, baby backs are the ribs to use, since they are smaller (2 pounds or less per rack) and are easy to cook. They do cook in less time and tend to be more tender than Spareribs. Baby backs should never have any chime bone or flap meat on them. If they do, they are most likely cheater ribs (St. Louis style trimmed to look like baby backs!) Baby backs are also the most expensive pork ribs you can buy! All baby back ribs should be curved in shape, because they are cut from the very top of the back of the animal.

Pork Butts, Shoulders or Picnics:

Pork butts and shoulders are the same type of meat, the picnic will contain the shank bone, where the butt is more towards the shoulder and will contain the blade bone. Using them with bone-in or boned is a matter of what you are going to do with it during the cooking process. I use the bone-in for a couple of reasons. First, the bone is a good test for when the butt is done and tender. The bone will easily slide out when the meat is ready and tender. Second, the meat cooked on the bone shrinks less. Removing the bone before smoking will reduce your cooking time and allow you to penetrate smoke flavor further into the meat. You will want to get your pork butt with the fat still on and then trim the fat to the thickness and amount that you prefer. **But** the fat is necessary for GREAT flavor!

Sausages:

I have found over the years that the best smoked sausage is what ever your personal tastes prefer. I do recommend that when smoking sausage, you buy bulk sausage, form it and smoke it without the casings. The casing will do two things; first it will sometimes block the smoke from penetrating the meat, and second, it can become tough!

Poultry:

I have found this to be one of the most fun meats to smoke and there are so many different birds to work with. When smoking breast, I like to use bone-in product. The bone controls shrinkage, helps retain moisture and adds flavor. The down side to the bone-in product is that you lose some smoke flavor on the bone side once your remove the meat from the bone, because the bone has absorbed the smoke and not allowed it to penetrated into the meat. But I have always found that the chicken breast will absorb enough smoke flavor on the other sides that it is worth the moisture retention. Bone-in product also increases the cooking time of the product. But again you need to weight the pros and cons! The items I have had the most fun with are:

Double Breast Bone-in Chicken
Whole Chickens (2-3 pound range)
Turkey Breast Bone-in (10-12 pound range)
Whole Turkey
Wild Whole Turkey
Quail
Pheasant
Duck Breast

Seafood:

My only caution here is the following rule: Learn your smoker and the DO's & DON'T's of smoking before moving into this category. The best products to smoke are fillets, which are bone free. Select fillets that are higher in fat content, since this will help keep the product moist during the smoking process. These are the fish that are considered darker meats. (i.e. trout, salmon, tuna, mackerel, bluefish) Most fillets of fish will need to be brined and air dried before smoking. Smoking seafood requires lots of attention, since all seafood tends to smoke very quickly. Trout, salmon and shrimp are the easiest to learn with.

These are also good products to add herbs to the smoker for additional flavors, since seafood lends itself well to the flavors of herbs. Once you know what you are doing, move into shrimp, scallops and lobster tail products for smoking as they are outstanding products for smoking. Shellfish takes time and more knowledge before attempting to smoke, so preoceed with care!
(See Secrets to Smoking Seafood page 47)

TIPS ON SMOKING MEATS

The smoking tips in this chapter are my own opinion from the many years of testing recipes in my smoker and information I have learned while competing and teaching smoking & BBQ classes. In this section I will just touch on the base meats used in smoking.

Brisket:

Whether smoking whole briskets, flats or points, smoke at a starting temperature of 200-225 degrees. The meat should be relaxed before placing in the smoker. This means you will want to let it sit at room temperature for at least an hour. My rule is to allow the brisket to sit out while I am building my fire and preheating my smoker. Rub can be placed on from 5 minutes before cooking to overnight, which really depends on the amount of salt in your rub. Remember, salt pulls moisture out of your product and moisture is one of the key factors in a great smoke ring and moist brisket. Smoke whole briskets (15-18 lbs.) for about 1 1/2 hours per pound. When cooking whole flats (7-10 lbs.) only, I apply 1 hour per pound cooking rule. Cook until an internal temperature of 195 degrees, remove from the smoker and wrap in foil then a towel or newspaper. Place the brisket in a cooler and allow it to cool down before slicing and serving. This allows the meat to relax, allowing the moisture to flow back through the entire fiber of the meat. Allow to rest for at least 20-30 minutes before serving.

Ribs:

I prefer to cook my ribs, whether spareribs or baby back ribs at a higher temperature. I smoke them at 230-250 degrees. This renders the fat out a little faster. Trim the ribs of any excess meat or fat. You will want your ribs to be the same thickness from end to end for more uniform cooking time and doneness. Peel the membrane from the back of the ribs before rubbing. I like to rub just a little bit of rub on the bone side and heavier rub on the meat side. I also rub my ribs about 4 hours before putting them in the smoker. Because I am using a higher temperature to smoke, I make sure I put my ribs in straight out of the refrigerator. This helps to build the smoke ring. The best way to tell if ribs are done is to use the "tear test". Take hold of two bones in the middle of the rib and pull them slightly. The meat should tear easily with a little bit of resistance to ensure the ribs are done.

Beef Tenderloin - whole:
Smoking whole tenderloin can be a rewarding event. Make sure that you leave a little bit of fat on the top of the whole tenderloin, since this beef product is very lean. If you are fully trimming the tenderloin, I suggest you rub it with olive oil before adding the dry rub or use a liquid marinade before smoking. The hardest part in smoking a whole tenderloin is to keep it from over cooking. I like to smoke my tenderloins until medium rare. Put the tenderloin in the smoker chilled but relaxed. For a medium rare smoked product, you will need to pull the tenderloin out at about 130 degrees, internal temperature. Let the tenderloin rest (covered) for at least 20-30 minutes before slicing.

Porkloins-boneless:
Marinating my pork loin in additional flavors is the way to go for me. Marinate for at least 12 hours before placing in the smoker. The most important thing to remember when doing a porkloin is to not over cook it. I recommend using a temperature probe, so that you can remove the loin before it over cooks. Place the probe directly through he center of the loin from the end side. Smoke at 225-230 degrees until the internal temperature reaches about 145 degrees. Remove from the smoker, place on a platter or dish and cover loosely for about 30-45 minutes. The carry over heat will continue to cook the loin another 5-10 degrees. Also, the resting of the meat will achieve a moist product.

Pork Butts or Picnics:
Buy your pork butts or picnics whole with the bone in and not trimmed. It is easier to trim the fat down yourself. The bone adds good flavor while it smokes, plus the bone is a natural thermometer, for shredded pork. When the bone pulls away free and clean the pork is fully cooked and tender enough for shredding. Deboning the pork butt is a easy process, and can be done by just following the meat down the sides of the bone and removing it. There is also a small gland on the opposite top side of the blade bone, just underneath the fat cap, it is about the size of a nickel and is easily removed with a boning knife.

I like to remove the first fat cap on top of the pork butt and the meat deckle right underneath this fat cap. This will get you down to the last layer of fat before the outside of the pork butt. This deckle is not very big and is only about 1/4" thick.

Italian Sausage:

I like to use bulk sausage that I can free form into a nice long cylinder shaped sausage about 2" thick in diameter. Wrap the log of sausage in saran wrap and roll tight, as if the saran was acting as a casting. Twist the ends tight to pack the sausage tightly into the saran. Keep the sausage very cold. When smoking, remove from the saran wrap and sprinkle well with a good dry rub and then place in the smoker. The reason I like to do this is that the castings on links can tend to block the smoke and worst yet, tend to get tough during the smoke cooking.

Chicken:

Chicken can be done as half chickens, quarter parts, bone-in breasts or bone-in thighs. I mention only bone-in, because your product will cook up better if left on the bone. It keeps the shrink ratio down, helps to retain moisture and add flavor. Brining can also improve the moisture of smoked poultry. (See Brining Poultry page 43). I like to smoke my chicken at a much higher temperature, around 275-300 degrees. Do not over smoke your chicken or use to much rub. Let the flavor of the rub compliment the chicken and not over power it. Make sure to rinse the chicken with fresh lemon water before prepping. This helps remove any bone bacteria that has build up in the product.

Turkeys:

I love doing turkeys in several different ways, whole, bone-in breasts, thighs and legs. Turkey is one of the few products I like to brine over night to really infuse it with some outstanding flavors. It is also one of the only products I like to inject before smoking. I recommend that you use the same brining solution for the injection. Make sure that before you brine the product, you reserve some of the clean brine for injecting.

You do not want to use brine that the turkey has sat in for the injection. I recommend brining whole turkeys for 24 hours. Breasts and thighs I brine for 12 hours. Always make sure that you rinse the turkey products well before doing any brining.

Special Note:

All poultry products should be rinsed in a lemon juice water solution, before preparing. The acid water helps remove any bacteria that builds up on the bone. It also helps to remove any blood smell from inside the body cavity.

BRINING POULTRY

We have all experienced chicken or turkey that really tasted dry, tough and chewy after smoking. Brining may be the one solution that can help you solve these problems. I believe in brining all my poultry items before smoking, I think it leads to a better product, both from moisture and flavor stand point.

Brining is a chemical action, but it is a simple action that only involves three things for it to happen.

Osmosis: By submerging meats into a liquid with a salt, the meat absorbs the liquid.

Protein Modification: The salt in the brining liquid changes the meat proteins, causing the proteins to change and trap excess water in the meat. The protein breaks down slightly allowing the flavorings and salt to penetrate in the meat.

Salt: It dissolves the protein, causing the meat to trap in more moisture.

Combine all three things and the result is a reduced amount of moisture loss during the smoking or cooking process ending with a juicer, tender and more flavorful product. Brining meat can help the cooking product retain up to 93% of its original weight versus an untreated product which can retain only about 85% of its original weight.

A simple rule for making a brine is the ratio of 2 quarts of water to 1/2 cup of salt. Always use kosher salt when brining. It is has no additives and is larger, which makes it less dense in weight than the same amount of table salt. It also makes your brine flavor more consistent.

You can substitute other liquids for the water, but remember to stay away from making the solution to acidic. Brines use osmosis to add moisture, while marinades use acid to tenderize. If you do add acid to the brine, reduce your brining time.

How long to brine?

It depends on the size of your item and the strength of the brine solution. Here is a guide chart for brining poultry items. These are sample times, so experiment and keep good notes for future changes and flavors.

Basic Brining Chart for Poultry

Weight of Item	**Brining Time**
Whole Chicken (3 lbs.)	6-8 hours
Chicken Thighs	90 minutes
Chicken Breast (bone-in)	60 minutes
Whole Turkey (12-15 lbs.)	24 hours
Turkey Breast (bone-in)	6-8 hours
Cornish Hens (whole)	2-3 hours

Always rinse your product off well before cooking, additional rubs or spices can be a put on after rinsing and patting dry.

Never reuse a brine that has had any food in it! Always brine under refrigeration (40° or below) and keep the container sealed to keep the air off your product.

SECRETS OF SMOKING SEAFOOD

RIB STARS®

What Makes For Top Quality Seafood?

How to Judge Fresh Raw Seafood:

By Odor - good, fresh fish does not have any strong odor. If a fish has a real "fishy" smell in the raw stage then, in all probability, it is not fresh. This same fish cooked will have an objectionable unappetizing odor.

By Feel - good, fresh fish should feel fairly firm -- not soft and mushy...it should never have a slimy feel.

By Taste - A strong, fish taste will exist when fish is not fresh. Good, fresh fish has a sweet, mild taste -- even the strong-flavored, high-fat fish, such as Mackerel, are sweet in flavor when truly fresh.

Fresh frozen fish is of prime importance...By this, I mean not only fresh caught fish in season, but FRESH FROZEN FISH that has been selected and frozen at the peak of its season. Frozen fish is like any other frozen food -- it must be handled with care. It must be thawed properly and given the same care as fresh-caught fish, with respect to storage in ice. It must be cooked and served as soon as possible after defrosting . Freezing, itself, does not cause off-flavors in fish. It is the handling before and after freezing that causes the deterioration.

Know What You Want and Where to Find It

Most important when buying seafood. KNOW YOUR SELLER!!! Ask your store about the product, don't assume because it is in the fresh counter that it was always fresh. Beware of the thawed frozen seafood, for it can tend to be old fish. Properly frozen and thawed seafood, can be excellent to use for smoking. Find out when it came to the store. Where did it come from? How long have they had it? Once you find a good source stick with the source for consistent product, be loyal to them and they will take care of your needs. Use the afore mentioned keys for quality seafood. This is the key when buying. Only buy what you really need for that dinner or function. You can always buy more later.

Most fish varieties are available fresh. Most of your shellfish items (i.e.. lobster tails, shrimp, crablegs) are not available fresh unless you live right on the coast.

Proper Storage:
Remove seafood from its packaging or container.

Carefully lay out the fish on a two inch deep perforated pan.

Place the perforated pan with the fish inside a deeper pan to allow for adequate drainage.

Cover the fish fillets with flaked (crushed) ice, filling the perforated pan full, so fillets will be completely covered with ice, and the ice flakes fall down through the fish fillets.

Place the pans of iced fish in the coldest part of the refrigerator immediately.

As the ice melts during the day, re-ice and drain bottom pan as necessary. Icing the fish with keep the flavor of the fish and fresher for up to two days without any odor developing. Change the pan each day to remove the water from the melting ice.

Thawing Your Frozen Seafood:
Only thaw frozen seafood for cooking two ways:
Method #1: Under refrigeration in a drain style pan, so that it will not sit in water as it it thawing. Change the pan daily until the product is completely thawed.

Method #2: If in a hurry it is acceptable to thaw frozen seafood under cold running water. Making sure the water is continuously running until seafood is thawed.

These are and should be the ONLY method used when thawing seafood!!

Preparing Seafood for Smoking:

While qualities of seafood varies from textures and flavors, almost any species of seafood can be smoked. This section focuses on the methods of smoking and preparation needed for smoking.

There are basically two different methods of smoking: hot smoking and cold smoking.

Hot smoking requires that the product be processed at temperatures between 140° to 225°. Hot smoked foods will last several days if stored under refrigeration. Longer if sealed in cryovac bags.

Cold smoking is a special low temperature cooking, also usually used as curing method. The product is cured and smoked at temperatures between 70 degrees and 90 degrees for prolong periods of time. This requires a special humidity and bacteria controlled smoker. Hence, I believe the cold smoking should be left to the professionals unless you have been fully trained to do this process and have the proper equipment.

The length of holding time varies depending on the brines salt and acid strength or the amount of salt used in the curing process.

All seafood should be cleaned and washed carefully before any processing is done, whether it is by brining or curing.

When brining or curing seafood only pure salt should be use, that is why I recommend using Kosher Salt or Sea Salt, never use regular table salt for either of these methods. Table salt has additives in it and will cause a bitter tasting product.

The size of the seafood will effect the cutting preparation and the final decision in what you are trying to achieve in your finished product. Small fish can be smoked whole or butterflied. Medium size fish can be smoked whole or filleted. Larger fish, can be smoked whole, but I recommend filleting the sides and possibly cutting the fillets into smaller portions.

Brining Seafood:

A brine is a salt solution (I prefer Kosher Salt and Filtered Water) which is used to increase the moisture content of the product. This will of coarse add additional flavors to the smoked product. Never use any form of aluminum pans or containers for this method, since these can cause an off flavor from a reaction to the metals.

Brining helps to:

* Firm up the flesh of the seafood
* Adds up to 20% more moisture to your product
* It will add the proper saltiness to your product
* It will draw out any off flavor (blood), improving the flavor
* It infuses additional flavors to your product
* It can also add additional color to your finished product

I like to use a smaller ratio of salt to water when brining and then brine for longer periods of time. I also prefer to start my brines with hot water and salt, this helps to dissolve the salt, and then cool down the brine before using it. I believe this infuses a better flavor into your product.

Basic Brine for Seafood

1 quart Water, hot
1 quart Water cold
1/2 cup of Kosher Salt or Sea Salt
1/2 cup Granulated Sugar or Brown Sugar

This is a standard brine, from here you can additional flavors such as garlic, onion juice, fruit juices or spices. Using hot water will help dissolve the salt and sugar faster. Once dissolved, add the cold water to cool the brine down before using. Make sure if you use garlic or onion salt that you figure the flavored salt into the salt ratio of the brine. When adding citrus juices, do not allow your brine to become aciditic, to avoid this, I believe in doing a 50/50 ratio of fruit juice to water to control the acid level of the brine. Too high of an acid level can make your protein set before cooking and you will end up with a mushy product.

Basic Brining Chart for Seafood

Weight of Fish Portions	Brining Time
4 ounces	30 minutes
8 ounces	1 hour
14-16 ounces	2-3 hours
1 1/2 to 2 pounds	4-5 hours
3-4 pounds	8 hours

Air Drying:

After brining, rinse the product in fresh cold water. Pat dry with paper towels and place the seafood on a wire rack and air dry for about 1-2 hours. Making sure that the product has plenty of space for air movement. Dry the seafood until the "pellicle" has formed. This is a thin shiny skin that helps the smoke evenly coat the surface and helps seal in the juices or "milk" of the seafood. When the fish is properly done it will feel smooth to the fingers. If the fish is smoked before this process, the moisture will leak out in a creamy white fluid that will actually sour during the cooling or storage process.

Smoking Times:

Depending on your seafood product the times and temperatures will vary. It is my belief that if you apply the rule of 1 hour for every 1 inch of thickness (at the deepest point) for proper and safe cooking times. (This is based on smoking temperature of 200 degrees). Always check your internal temperature properly before eating. A lower temperature of 180°adds about another 15 minutes per 1 inch of thickness and a higher temperature of 225°can reduce your time by 15 minutes per 1 inch of thickness. **But** always cook until the proper internal temperature of 145 degrees is reached. At a temperature of 145 degrees, your seafood is fully cooked and is still moist and flaky. Remember that all items that are cooked will continue to cook after it is removed from the smoker, this cooking heat is called "carry over heat".

The length of the smoking time can be from 30 minutes for small fillets of catfish or scallops, to 2 hours for a 3 pound side of salmon. An average side of salmon (fillet) weighting 3 pounds, will be fully cooked in 2 hours. From here you can smoke longer if you wish to achieve a dry smoke salmon or jerky style.

Seafood Smoking Time

Weight of Seafood	Approx. Smoking Time
1/4 to 1/2 pound	30- 45 minutes
1/2 to 1 pound	45 -60 minutes
1 to 2 pounds	1 to 1 1/2 hours
2 to 3 pounds	1 1/2 to 2 hours
3 to 4 pounds	2 1/2 to 3 hours

I generally smoke my seafood at 200 degrees. Lower or higher temperatures can be used with a corresponding adjustment to the smoking time. The seafood is done when it reaches an internal temperature
of 145 degrees.

The follow seafoods are some of my favorite selections and some of the easier items to start with.

Bluefish:
Higher in oil and fat content, but makes a nice flavored smoked fish. The use of fresh ground black pepper once the fillet is brined and dried, adds a nice flavor to this higher fat content fish. Also, once smoked, bluefish makes an outstanding spread.

Lobster Tails:
Save the best for last. There is nothing like a smoked cold water lobster tail. Use the same methods as you would shrimp, but because of the size and weight different, brine the tails for at least one hour, air dry and hot smoke for about 2 - 2 1/2 hours.

Marlin:
Easy to hot smoke and provides a very different and distinct flavor. Although the meat of this fish is dark red, it will become light pink after it is smoked.

Oysters & Clams:
If you like these items, you will love them smoked! Both oysters and clams need to be shucked before brining. Brine them for about 10 minutes or more and then air dry as you would other seafood. Oysters and clams absorb smoke more rapidly than other seafoods.

Salmon & Trout:
These two fish lend themselves very well to the beginner. I find that these fish are nicely smoked using the brine and hot smoke methods. Use them both in the boneless fillet preparation. Salmon is best when smoked in whole sides, skinless and boneless. Trout smokes well in a whole butteflied and boneless preparation.

Scallops:
This is one of my favorite items to smoke! If done properly they create the most flavorful golden nuggets of sweetness. Matched in flavor by no other seafood item. Use only the bigger scallops (at least 1" in diameter) to keep from over cooking them.

Shrimp:

What an outstanding item. If you love shrimp, you have got to try smoking them. Shrimp needs only about 45 to 60 minutes of brining. Make sure to peel the shrimp before brining and smoking. If you don't, the skin will trap moisture between the meat and the shell which will make the shrimp become tough. And of course, the shell will absorb too much of the smoke.

Tuna:

Provides some challenges, but once mastered it makes for excellent smoked product. Plus, the tuna can be smoke as a whole loin piece like a pork loin and slices nice. Make sure whoever cuts the loin fillet for you removes the dark lateral band from the inside of the loin. This band of dark meat imparts a very bitter flavor to the surrounding meat.

These are only some of the easier items to learn with, but the list of seafood to smoke only stops when you want it to. Remember that the times for length of smoking will vary depending on the size of

the product, type of smoker used and temperature that you are smoking at.

Special Tips on Brining & Smoking Seafood:

Buying- Buy the FRESHEST product you can find.

Rinse- All fish fillets or portions well in clean cold water. Before brining.

Water for brining- I always like to use filtered or bottled water when starting my brine solutions.

Salt for brining- I prefer only Kosher or Sea salts for the brining solutions. They are pure and have no additives.

Log Sheets- Always keep a record of what you did from start to finish. Keeping as much information as you possible can about the seafood, brine, brining time, drying time and method.

Wood & Time- Use a milder wood when doing seafood, do not over smoke. Let your wood burn well before placing your product in the smoker. You want a clean smoke, not a smoldering smoke. Log your times for future notes on smoking. Do not over smoke the product.

Storage- Using a vacuum sealer will extend the shelf life of your smoked product up to 50%. It also helps keep the product intact while storage and handling.

TEMPERATURES
&
TIMES

Absolute cooking times in smoking are nearly impossible. Wind, cold weather, hot weather, sunshine, clouds and rain will effect the length of the cooking time.

The best method for cooking is to track the weather and method used on the day of cooking. I like to log all important facts of the process.

Wind can lead to faster cooking times or even worse inconsistent heat. Arrange your smoker in position to use the wind to your benefit. By changing the position of the smoker you can control the speed of the wind flowing through the vents of your smoker.

Sunshine will decrease your cooking times up to 25%. Cold weather or cloudiness may increase your smoking time from 30% to 50%, depending on how severe the weather or temperature may be.

Rain is the most difficult to deal with, since it not only creates excess moisture, but also continually cools the temperature of your smoker. I have found that if you can produce a great product in the rain, you will be successful in any weather. Hence, I tend to do a lot of my smoking and test recipes in the rain.

I like to preheat my smoker to 300°before I put my product in the smoker. Once in the smoker, I allow it to cool down to my desired smoking temperature. I have found that this produces an excellent outer crust or "BBQ bark". The high starting temperature allows for this temperature loss when loading your products and keeps your smoker at a safe range, without having to heat back up to temperature after the meat has be place in the smoker.

The following pages gives some good examples of cooking times for the more common cuts of meat.

SMOKE CHART:

FOOD ITEM	HEAT RANGE	APPROXIMATE COOKING TIME
Brisket Flat (8-10 pounds)	200°	8-10 hours
Beef Ribs (3 lbs. slabs)	250-275°	6 hours
Chicken Breast (10 oz. bone-in)	275-300°	1.5 hours (or 165°)
Whole Chicken (3 pounds)	275-300°	2-2.5 hours (or 165°)
Turkey Breast (10-12 pounds bone in)	250-275°	5-6 hours (or 165°)
Whole Turkey (12-15 pound)	275-300°	6-7 hours (or 165°)
Pork Butt (8-10 pound)	200°	10-12 hours (until "pulled")
Pork Tenderloin (1 pound)	225°	2 hours
Pork Ribs (Spareribs 3 lbs.)	250°	6 hours
Pork Ribs (Baby Back 1 1/2 lbs.)	250°	4 hours

SMOKE CHART:

FOOD ITEM	HEAT RANGE	APPROXIMATE COOKING TIME
Trout Fillets (boneless)	200°	30 minutes
Catfish Fillets (boneless & skinless)	200°	30 minutes
Salmon Fillets (sides)	200°	1 1/2 - 2 hours
Lobster Tails	200°	2 hours
Scallops (1" diameter)	200°	45 minutes
Shrimp (16/20 ct.)	200°	45 minutes

*Remember times will vary, depending on outdoor temperature, weather conditions, plus style and size of smoker. All temperatures are based on a dry smoker using lump coal and wood.

Proper Internal Temperatures for Doneness:
Cook all food to the safe internal temperature for that product, to ensure that bacteria, present in all foods, are destroyed.
The proper internal temperatures by food product are:
(as issued by the Food and Drug Administration/Food Codes)

Whole Beef & Lamb: 145°
Pork: 145°
Seafood: 145°
Poultry: 165°
Ground Beef: 155°
Ground Poultry: 155°

TO WRAP
OR
NOT TO WRAP

The GREATEST question in the BBQ world today is whether or not you should wrap your meats during smoking or not, and whether it should be done with aluminum foil or saran!

I am going to address the positives and the negatives of each way and I believe that each person needs to decide what their choice is. There is no right or wrong when it comes to this issue, there is only opinions of what each person who smokes believes in.

Wrapping is really a matter of reducing cooking time and to make the product tender at a quicker rate. You can produce very good smoked briskets, pork butts or ribs without wrapping. A unwrapped product will take a longer time to cook than a wrapped product. Watched right, you will still have a moist tender product. Not wrapping your product also allows you to be able to mop your products longer, which is a positive advantage point of not wrapping.

Wrapping your product should be done for the following reasons:

- You have achieved the perfect meat color and smoke flavor you want and do not want the product to get over smoked.
- You are tandem smoking and want to use several different woods to flavor your products, by wrapping each product as you add a different item you can change your wood flavors with each item.
- You are on a tight schedule and would like to reduce the amount of smoking time.
- You want to achieve tenderness of the product at a faster pace than unwrapped method.
- You are having problems achieving tenderness in your smoke products.

Once you have decided on whether or not you want to wrap for any reason, now you should decide on what wrap to use! One thing to remember is to allow all wrapped meat to cool down while it is still wrap, I like to open the top of the wrapped product, creating a 2" vent to allow the excess steam to escape. The cool down period while wrapped will also allow the product to absorb back some of the lost moisture. The remaining juices can also be used to pour over the sliced or shredded product when serving.

If you decide to wrap your products there are only three ways to go. Foil wrapped, saran wrapped or wrapped with saran and then foil. All three methods will tend to steam the meat and soften the bark.

Foil does not shrink as it cooks, allowing the meat room inside. Because it does not shrink as it cooks, it will not put any pressure on the meat, therefore keeping in extra juices that are needed for a moist product. It is the easiest method to deal with when unwrapping.

Saran wrap tends to steam the meat more than foil. Saran also shrinks in long periods of high heat, as it shrinks it tightens on the meat and forces more juices from the meat product. Some saran wraps I found, will sometimes start to crack at 195 degrees. The positive on saran wrap is that by steaming the meat, it will tenderize faster from the steam trapped in the package. I recommend cooling the meat with the top open slightly to release excess steam. I would then place the meat back in the smoker unwrapped to dry out the meat a little from the steam.

Some like to wrap with saran and then foil. The only advantage I have found for this is that foil, sometimes tears when you are moving it, which is why I like to double foil wrap my products. Saran will protect the juices if the foil tears, but again, I go back to the disadvantages of saran on the cooking meat product.

So! We are back to the beginning topic of whether you want to wrap or not. It is entirely up to you! **<u>You</u>** should decide based on the information you now have what your choice is **<u>and</u>** your final choice should be whatever method gives you the finished product you are looking for! **That is the REAL reason to wrap or not wrap!**

Remember to allow all wrapped products to cool down in the package before slicing or serving!

SPICES & HERBS

This section touches on some of the more common spices and herbs used in cooking. This list is not the final word on spices, as there are many combinations you can try and hundreds of different spices and herbs to test and learn about. This list is just a starting point!

Spices:

Allspice:
Small berry, the size of a pea, dried to dark brown. Has an aroma similar to a mixture of cloves, cinnamon and nutmeg. Used whole in pickling, cooking meats and fish. Used ground in cakes, puddings and preserves.

Anise:
Small dried ripe fruit of annual herb. Has flavor of licorice. Used in Chinese sauces.

Caper:
Flower bud. Used in salad dressings and fish sauces.

Caraway Seed:
ried ripe fruit of an herb of the parsley family. Used in breads. Compliments itself well with pastrami style meats.

Cardamon:
Dried miniature fruit of a tropical bush. Used to achieve certain Hawaiian or Polynesian flavors.

Cayenne:
Small hot red peppers, ground fine. Used in meats, stews and sauces. Adds heat to rubs and seasonings.

Celery Seed:
Dried seed like fruit of an herb of the parsley family. Has the flavor of celery. Used in meat and fish dishes, salads and salad dressings.

Chili Powder:
Ground chili pepper pods and blended spices. Very hot flavor. Used in chili con carne and other Mexican dishes. Good for rubs.

Cinnamon:
Thin inner bark of cinnamon tree. Used in stick form and ground for fruits and preserves.

Clove:
Dried flower buds of clove tree grown in East Indies. Used whole in meats, pickling and fish.

Coriander:
Dried ripe fruit of an herb of the parsley family. Used whole in pickle, poultry stuffing and green salads. Used ground in sausages or on fresh pork.

Cumin Seed:
Small dried fruit of a plant belonging to the parsley family. Used whole in soups, cheese spreads, stuffed eggs, stews and sausage. Used ground as an ingredient in curry and chili powder. Excellent in certain dry rubs.

Dill Seed:
Small dark seed of dill plant, grown in India. Sharp taste resembling caraway seed. Used in pickles, sauces, salad, soups and stews.

Ginger:
Root of plant resembling the iris, grown in India. Root (cracked) used in chutney, pickles, preserves and dried fruit.

Mace:
Orange red fleshy covering of nutmeg kernel, grown on nutmeg trees in Indonesia. Used in fish sauces, pickling, preserving.

Nutmeg:
Dried, hard, wrinkled seed or pit of nutmeg fruit, grown in Indonesia. Aromatic, slightly bitter flavor. Used whole, grated as needed. Used ground in sausage.

Paprika:
Dried, ripe red pepper grown in middle Europe, United States and Chile. Pleasant odor, mild sweet flavor. Used to season shellfish and to color meats. Used in dry rubs.

Pepper (Peppercorn):
Dried small round berry of tropical vine with small white flowers, extensively grown in India. Used whole in pickling, meats and stews. Used ground for general seasonings of meats, fish, poultry, vegetables and salads.

White Pepper:
Mature berry with black coat removed (usually ground). White pepper is used in dishes that require a less pungent flavor than that given by black pepper.

Poppy Seed:
Tiny, dark gray seeds of poppy plant, grown in the United States and Turkey. Used in some sweet and sour sauces and in infusing oils for salads.

Sesame Seed:
Small, flat, oily seed of sesame plant. Used in infusing oils for marinating and for flavors in Oriental cooking.

Mustard:
Small, round seeds of an annual herb bearing yellow flowers. Pungent flavor. Dry mustard used in meat, sauces, gravies, salad dressings. Used ground in dry rubs.

Turmeric:
Ground dried aromatic root of turmeric plant, grown in the Orient. Slightly bitter flavor. Used ground in curry powder, meat and egg dishes.

Fresh Herbs:

Angelica:
Green plant, grown in the United States. Leaves and stalks used in flavoring liqueurs. Used in combination with Juniper berries.

Basil:
Dried small leaves of a herbaceous plant. Used in stews, soups and egg dishes.

Bay Leaf: Dried, aromatic small shiny leaves of laurel tree. Used in soups, chowders, stews, fish, tomatoes and pickles.

Dill:
The fine leaves of the plant are used fresh or dried. The seeds are dried. Seeds are a must for making pickles. Lends itself well to mixing with softened butter for topping seafood dishes.

Fennel:
Feather leaves which must be used fresh, but the seeds can be dried and ground. Licorice flavored. Either leaves or seeds can enrich, soups, stuffing, sausages and root vegetables.

Lemon Balm:
Soft feathery leaves. Has the look of large mint leaves, nice lemon flavor. Adds an extra lemony flavor to herb butters for seafood dishes. Great with Scallops.

Marjoram:
Dried leaves and flowering tops of aromatic plant of the mint family. Used fresh in salads. Used dried in meat and poultry seasoning.

Mint:
Leaves of spearmint plant, grown almost everywhere. Used fresh for beverages. Used dried in sauces.

Oregano:
Dried leaves of a perennial herb of the mint family. Aromatic odor, slightly bitter flavor. Used dried in tomato sauces, pork and egg dishes. Used as an ingredient in chili powder.

Parsley:
Two forms of fresh; curly leaf and flat leaf. Has a subtle pungency flavor that survives cooking. Good in stuffing and casseroles. Mainly used as a garnish of food. Adds color to spice blends.

Rosemary:
An evergreen shrub. Pungent. Compliments, lamb, beef and pork the best. Used in marinades to infuse flavors

Saffron:
Dried stigma of a perennial plant closely resembling the crocus, grown chiefly in Spain, France and Italy. Very expensive. Used mainly for its yellow color.

Sage:
Dried leaves of a perennial shrub of the mint family. Used dried in sausage, meat products, fowl and stuffing.

Savory:
Dried leaves and flowering tops of an annual herb. Used fresh to flavor soups, salads, sauces and gravies. Used dried in stuffing, salad dressings and stews.

Tarragon:
Dried leaves and flowering tops of an aromatic herb, native to Siberia. An ingredient used in vinegar to develop special flavor. Used in fish sauces.

Thyme:
Dried leaves and flowering tops of an annual herb with purple flowers, cultivated extensively in central Europe. Used dried in soups, sauces, stuffing and cheese. Used ground in rubs.

BASICS OF A DRY RUB

THE "FOUR" FLAVOR STAGES OF A DRY RUB

A good rub must have an equal balance of flavors. Typically a rub should consist of four flavor stages. The flavor profile of each stage may be adjusted to your own personal taste.

Stage 1: Sweet/Salt - This stage is the beginning stage and should be a balance between the salts and sugar used. Usually this stage is made up of equals parts. I only use Kosher Salt in my rubs, for it has a truer flavor and has no additives. For the sugars, I use granulated brown sugar or turbinado (natural raw sugar). Turbinado sugar can take a higher temperature before it burns, so it is a better sugar for dry rubs.

Stage 2: Color - This stage is just that, adding color to the rub to define the deepness of reds in your rubs. I use Paprika and Chili Powder for my color stage. (I personally do not use Chili Powder as my heat source, but I use it more for a coloring point).

Stage 3: Heat - Be careful in this stage, since this is where you can make your rubs too hot in heat degrees of flavor. I like to use Black Pepper, Cayenne Pepper and White Pepper. The tri-mix of peppers makes a good heat flavor combination.

Stage 4: Flavorings - In this stage you can add a lot of your own personal taste. I recommend starting out with Garlic and Onion Powders (not salts) because they add true flavor. I also put Lemon Pepper in my flavoring stage (more lemony than pepper). From there, it is a matter of personal taste! I like cumin, poultry seasoning, ground oregano, ground thyme, etc. Use your sense of smell and taste to your liking. Remember that the flavoring spice must match well with the meat product you are going to use it on. I like to test the selected spices on some cooked meat before I use it in a rub. That is why I have several different rubs for beef, pork and chicken.

When testing your rubs always remember to change only one ingredient at a time, so you know will what item changed the flavor!

The standard rule to follow in making a rub is: 4 parts Stage 1, 2 parts Stage 2, 1 part Stage 3 and 1 part Stage 4!

Once you have developed your "secret" rub, your friends will envy your BBQ and come back for more!

MAKING BBQ SAUCE

Whether you use your barbecue sauce to mop or to sop your meat while at the picnic table, there are some main factors to decide before making your sauce.

First! What style are you looking for? There are several different styles of barbecue sauces. Kansas City style which is a thicker tomato based sauce, which tends to be sweet and spicy with a little heat. Texas style sauces are also tomato based, but are thinner and have more of a distinctive bite from worcestershire sauce and a touch of molasses. The Carolina's can have a range of three to four different styles. Most of the Carolina's are thin sauces, some tomato based, some vinegar based and others mustard based. Several of them are on the sweet and sour side, using vinegar and sugar. You will find some areas are a combination of several types, Florida uses a tomato base, but for the acid side they use lime and lemon juice. Kentucky sauces are known as black sauces, mostly made from worcestershire sauce and vinegar. As I have travel around, I taste as many barbecue sauces as I can. I am always amazed at the flavors of sauces in just one region. There is even Hawaiian style sauces, which I like to refer to them as fruit sauces, since most of them have fruit juices in them.

Second! Decide on the flavor and profile of your sauce. Do I want it sweet? Spicy? Maybe I want it to be sweet and spicy with some heat to it. Do I want to add some sour to it for a certain flavor?

Third! Develope your ingredient list. Make sure you can get what you are looking for in your area.

Fourth! Making and testing your sauce. Keep good notes on what you did. Measure correctly and well. Taste your final product and determine what you like or maybe don't like. When going back to retest, **only change one ingredient at a time!** That way you know what causes the change. If you change more than one, you will not know what made your sauce change for the final taste.

When making barbecue sauces, everyone has his or her twist or beliefs to making a good barbecue sauce. Here are some of my guidelines or rules that I like to follow when testing and making a new sauce.

Tomato Stage:
Tomato puree - ground tomatoes with sauce.
Tomato paste - tomato meats cooked down to thick paste.
Ketchup - tomato puree with vinegar, sweeteners and spices.
Chili Sauce - tomato puree with onions, garlic and spices.

Sweet Stage:
The following are different products to use to make your sauce have some sweetness to it.

Granulated sugar, light or dark brown sugar, turbinado sugar, honey, light or dark corn syrups, maple syrup, jellies, molasses, soda and sorghum just to list a few.

Sour Stage:
You will want to make sure that in this stage that you don't add all of the sour product at once. I like to just add only half the amount of sour I am using at a time. You don't want your sauce to become to pungent.

White or flavored vinegars, lemon juice and lime juice.
Vinegars come in numerous flavors, so when using vinegars you can add additional flavors to your sauce.

Other liquids:
These can be added for flavoring or thinning your sauce.
Worcestershire sauce, fruits juices, fruit nectars, horseradish, liquid smoke, mustard, hot sauce, soft drinks, beef or chicken broths, beer and tomato juice.

Seasonings: *(see Spices & Herbs page 66 for flavor profiles)*
Almost all barbecue sauces have salt, pepper (black, red, or white) and chili powder. From there you can add any spice you like. Again, know the profile of the seasoning before adding it to your sauce.

Production Stage:

Once you have made you decision on the other stages, you can now start your sauce production. Make sure to use a nonreactive pan. I like to combine all my ingredients in the sauce pan first before going to the heat. Combine your spices, chili powder and peppers in the flavoring liquid or worcestershire sauce first, making a loose paste. This insures that the powders and spices are dissolve well, before adding them to your sauce. This also helps to keep them from forming lumps. Then add your other liquids, remembering only start with half of your sour liquids. Stir well, combining all the ingredients. Place the sauce pan on medium high heat and start to warm, stirring constantly. Bring the sauce to a boil, then reduce the heat and continue simmering until the sauce has reduced to the desired thickness. Before removing from the heat, taste the sauce, adjust the seasoning if needed and decide if you need the remaining sour in your sauce. If adding any sour or seasonings, continue cooking for 5 more minutes to incorporate the flavors. Remove from the heat.

Remember, your sauce is the finishing taste added to your barbecue. Whether it is put on during the last stage of cooking or if just used as a sop at the table. The sauce should complement your food, not over power it!

DO'S & DON'TS

RIB STARS®

DO:

Always have a clean burning fire and a non-smothering smoke before adding any product to your smoker.

Remove excessive bark from your wood. This helps reduce any harsh flavor in the product.

Allow the smoker to reach a internal temperature of 300° before placing any product in the chamber. This will account for the temperature drop when product is added.

Use the vents to control the heat needed to maintain the inner temperature.

Always add a little fuel at a time to insure proper burning of the fuel.

Always use any finishing sauce with tomato product at the end of the cooking process.

Always have a mop or spray available and ready for use when you open your smoker. My rule of thumb is once the bark is set, I spray or mop each time the smoker is open.

If wrapping your product, always allow the product to cool down while still wrapped. This will allow the product to absorb back some of the loss juices. Just create a small opening on the top about 2" in diameter to allow excess steam to release.

Clean your smoker of excessive fat drippings and build up each time you use your smoker. Excessive build up can create a harsh flavor and drippings left in your smoker can create a health hazard.

Clean your meat grills while still warm.

Enjoy yourself as you wait for the flavors of the day!

DON'T:

Add meat before building fire, this will put an awful harsh flavor in your meat.

Use any starter fluids to get your coals going. Start your fire the natural way (newspaper, starter chips or starter gel).

Close your top vent too much. This will smother your inner chamber with smoke and lead to a harsher flavor in your meats. (A lot of smoke is not a good sign of a great product!)

Open your smoker a lot as this will increase your smoking time. Only open your smoker to mop the meats or check for doneness! The meat is not going anywhere, relax!

Overload smokers so that product takes too long to cook. The smoker will lose temperature and smoke to fast and the air in the smoker will not be able to circulate properly.

Use a mop that has too much tomato product or sugar product. These products will burn before the meat is done, giving you a very bitter product.

Allow excessive build up in your smoker. This will also cause harsh flavors and could cause flare up.

Allow food products or drippings to stand in your smoker or grill racks. These can cause health hazards.

Pierce the meat product with a fork to test for doneness. This will allow important juices to escape, resulting in a drier and less flavorful product.

RECORDING & TESTING

I believe the most important part of developing great recipes for smoking, barbecuing or just cooking, is keeping good record or logs when testing and developing recipes.

On the next page is a Test Sheet I have created to help me log my trials and errors on my way to a finished and acceptable product.

I use these sheets for <u>every</u> new item I am creating! Once the item has been tested, I then write my recipe in the recipe log.

Everything I feel is important to a successful product is included on these sheets: weather, temperature, product used, product trim, fuel used, type of wood, cooking start time, finishing time, rubs, marinades, mops, sauces and special notes of the day.

I will even draw sketches of the food placement in my smoker.

Hourly, I log what the smoker temperature is and how the vents are set. And in the end, I make comments about how the product turned out!

The best thing is that these Test Sheets help improve the product as a whole. There is no guessing what you did and when you want to retest, you have all your information right there.

One of the <u>most</u> important things about retesting recipes for flavor is to never change more than one ingredient at a time, whether it is a rub spice, marinade or mop!! Changing more than one item at a time can confuse which item really made the final change in flavor. **This my biggest rule in testing new recipes!**

Example Test Sheet

SMOKER NOTES
DATE & WEATHER:
05/06/99 CLEAR AND WARM 75°

NEW ITEM NAME:
SMOKED BRISKET

A. TYPE OF MEAT & GRADE
BRISKET FLAP (CHOICE)

WEIGHT OF MEAT:
6 POUNDS

B. FAT TRIM OF MEAT:
1/4" TRIM

C. HEAT SOURCE:
LUMP COAL

AMOUNT OF SOURCE:
3 POUNDS

D. TYPE OF WOOD:
SUGAR MAPLE

PIECES OF WOOD USED:
3 - 2" PIECES.

E. TIME STARTED MEAT:
6:00 AM

COOKING TIME OF MEAT:
10 HOURS

F. DRY SEASONING USED:
RIB STARS BRISKET RUB

G. M.O.P. :
1. TERIYAKI SAUCE
2. YELLOW MUSTARD
3. CHILI PASTE
4. WHITE VINEGAR
5. PINEAPPLE JUICE
6. RUB SEASONING
7.

H. SAUCE USED: NONE

I. SPECIAL NOTES:

6:00 AM- PLACED BRISKET IN THE MIDDLE OF THE SMOKER, WITH SIDE VENT OPEN AND STACK FULLY OPENED. MEAT LEVEL TEMP. 210° MAINTAINED AND CHECKED TEMP. EVER HOUR.

9:00 AM - MOPPED BRISKET WITH MOP, FOR THE FIRST TIME. TEMP 225°. ADDED SOME WOOD, SIDE VENT HALF OPEN.

11:30 AM- MOPPED BRISKET AGAIN, TEMP 225°, ADDED COAL

1:30 P.M.- MOPPED BRISKET, TEMP 210°, ADDED COAL, MAYBE 1 POUND.

2:30 P.M.- CHECKED TEMP. 210°, ADDED MORE COAL.

3:30 P.M.- MOPPED BRISKET, ADDED COAL. TEMP. 225°, WRAPPED IN SARAN AND FOIL. CLOSED SIDE VENT TO 1/3, COOL DOWN TIME. TEMP. 190°

4:30 P.M. - REMOVED BRISKET, SLICE AND SERVED. SMOKER TEMP. 175°.

BRISKET WAS VERY GOOD IN FLAVOR, TENDERNESS WAS VERY GOOD. NEXT TIME REMOVE MORE FAT.

PERSONAL TIPS

TIP #1:
Use 100% lump coal. Lump coal lights faster and burns hotter, helping to make your fire heat last longer.

TIP #2:
Always test your smoker before cooking for the True Temperature at meat level. Run your outside gauge accordingly to achieve proper temperature inside your smoker.

TIP #3:
Remove as much bark as possible from the wood that you are using. I find that too much bark can make for a very harsh flavor in the meat.

TIP #4:
Allow foiled wrapped meats to rest in the foil, but allow some of the steam out of the wrap while cooling.

TIP #5:
Place your meat in your smoker as cool as possible, but relaxed. This will help develope a deeper absorption of smoke (smoke ring).

TIP #6:
Remember at 120 degrees internal temperature protein starts to set. At 140° the protein is completely set and can not absorb anymore smoke flavor.

TIP #7:
Only open your smoker to mop your products. Opening your smoker too much will increase your cooking time and allow your smoke to escape.

TIP #8:
To add some zip to your marinades or mops, try using Asian chile paste. Start with small amounts and increase slowly.

TIP #9:
Never allow your smoker to build up inside, as this leads to an off flavor of your product. I prefer to clean out my smoker and brush clean all the grills after each use. Completely clean and check your smoker for build up once a year.

TIP #10:
The use of dry herb branches are great for flavoring your smoke or liquid in your water pan. Rosemary, thyme or oregano branches are excellent. I like to add them to the water pan to infuse the moisture in the smoker chamber with additional flavor.

TIP #11:
Try using spray bottles for applying your mops. You will need to strain your mops. Your mops need to be thin enough to be able to go through the spray tube. Use fruit juice or nectars to thin your mop down.

TIP #12:
When testing and creating new items, make sure you record your notes and only change one thing at a time for successful retesting. Have patience and remember developing new items takes time.

BBQ Sauces

10-2-4 BBQ Sauce
Backyard Double "J" BBQ Sauce
Carolina BBQ Sauce
Chinese BBQ Sauce
"Take Your Breath Away" BBQ Sauce
Maple BBQ Sauce
Passion BBQ Sauce
Teriyaki BBQ Sauce
Whiskey BBQ Sauce

10-2-4 BBQ SAUCE

This is more of a Southern Vinegar Style Sauce.
Good vinegar & spicy flavor for sopping chicken, pulled pork or beef ribs.

2 cups	Tomato Sauce, canned
3/4 cups	Dr. Pepper®, canned
3/4 cups	White Vinegar
3/4 cups	Chili Sauce
3/4 cups	Karo Syrup, dark
1/4 cup	A-1® Steak Sauce
1/4 cup	Worcestershire sauce
2 TB.	Honey
2 TB.	Yellow Mustard
1 each	Juice of Lemons
1 TB.	Olive Oil
1 dash	Hot Sauce
1 TB.	Black Pepper, table grind
1 TB.	Garlic Salt
1 tsp.	Onion Salt

Combine all ingredients in a sauce pot, stirr and blend well. Bring the sauce to a boil and then reduce to a simmer. Simmer for 30 minutes to infuse all flavors. Store covered in refrigeration.

Makes: about 6 cups

BACKYARD DOUBLE "J" BBQ SAUCE

This sauce is on the sweet spicy side of BBQ sauces.

6 cups	Ketchup
1/2 cup	Brown Sugar, golden brown
3/4 cup	Corn Syrup, Light
1/2 cup	Honey
1/4 cup	Molasses
1/2 cup	Yellow Mustard, pourable
1/3 cup	White Vinegar
1/3 cup	Onion Juice
1/4 cup	Worcestershire sauce
3 TB.	Lemon Juice, fresh
2 TB.	Maggi Seasoning
2 TB.	Sparerib Rub (page 118)
1 tsp.	Celery Seed
2 tsp.	Liquid Smoke Flavoring
2 tsp.	Kitchen Bouquet®
1 tsp.	Black Pepper, table grind

Combine all ingredients together and blend well. Bring to a full boil, reduce and simmer for 1 1/2 hours or until slightly thickened. Remove from the heat and hold for service or cool completely and store in refrigerator until needed.

Makes: 2 quarts

CAROLINA BBQ SAUCE

My favorite version of a Carolina sauce that is great on pulled pork.

1/4 cup	Salad Oil
2 TB.	Shallot, minced
6 cloves	Garlic, fresh, minced
1 cup	Cider Vinegar
1 tsp.	Celery Seed
2 each	Cloves
1 TB.	Dry Mustard
1 tsp.	Chili Powder
1 tsp.	Pulled Pork Rub (page 117)
3/4 cup	Brown Sugar
1 1/2 cups	Ketchup
1/2 cup	Water
1 tsp.	Crushed Red Pepper Flakes

Heat oil in a sauce pan; add the minced shallots and minced garlic, cook until they just begin to brown. Add the vinegar, spices, dry mustard, brown sugar and ketchup. Stir to blend well. Add the water and stir well. Bring to a boil. Lower the heat to simmer, add salt and pepper to taste. Simmer for about 20 to 30 minutes.

Makes: about 1 quart.

CHINESE BBQ SAUCE

Use this sauce as a finish to ribs just before they are removed from the smoker.

1 TB.	Garlic, minced
6 TB.	Soy Sauce, lite
2 TB.	Plum Sauce
2 TB.	Black Bean Sauce
6 TB.	Hoisin Sauce
1 1/2 tsp.	Chinese 5 Spice
1 each	Star Anise, whole
1/2 cup	Brown Sugar, light
1/2 cup	Sherry
2 TB.	Cornstarch

Mix all ingredients together except for the sherry and cornstarch. Place the liquid over medium heat until hot. Once hot dissolve the cornstarch in the sherry and mix with the hot liquid. Continue heating until sauce comes to quick boil and thickens. Remove the sauce from the heat and remove the star anise from the sauce, hold warm for service or refrigerate until needed.

Makes: about 3 cups.

"TAKE MY BREATH AWAY" BBQ SAUCE

Breathe some life into your pork ribs with this sauce!

6 cups	Ketchup
1/2 cup	Horseradish, hot, prepared
1 cup	Chicken Broth, canned
1 cup	White Vinegar
1/2 cup	Corn Syrup, light
1 TB.	Dry Mustard
1 cup	Brown Sugar, golden brown
2 TB.	Shallot, minced
1 cup	Worcestershire Sauce
4 TB.	Hot Sauce
1 1/2 TB.	Kosher Salt
1 TB.	Pulled Pork Rub (page 117)
2 ounces	Kitchen Bouquet®
5 TB.	Pick-a-Pepper Sauce, brown
2 tsp.	Black Pepper, table grind

Make a paste of the Worcestershire Sauce and dry mustard. Combine all the rest of the ingredients together and add the paste to the mixture, blend well. Bring to a boil and simmer for 1 hour to reduce slightly. DO NOT ALLOW THE SAUCE TO SCORCH!

Remove from the heat and hold warm for service or cool completely and store in the refrigerator until needed.

Makes: 2 1/2 quarts

MAPLE BBQ SAUCE

A nice sweet flavor from the maple syrup with a little kick from the Worcestershire Sauce.

2 cups	Maple Syrup, "Real"
2 cups	Ketchup
1 cup	White Onions, minced
1/2 cup	Corn Syrup, light
1/2 cup	Apple Cider
1 cup	Water
4 TB.	Butter
4 TB.	Worcestershire Sauce
1 TB.	Garlic, fresh, minced
1 tsp.	Kosher Salt
1 tsp.	Hot Sauce

Melt the butter in a sauce pan add the onions and saute until transparent. Add all the ingredients to the onions. Stir to blend well. Bring to a boil and reduce the heat. Simmer for 20 minutes and remove from the heat.

Makes: 7 1/2 cups.

PASSION BBQ SAUCE

An excellent spicy fruit sauce, outstanding on poultry and seafood!

4 cups	Chili Sauce
1 cup	Corn Syrup, light
1 cup	White Vinegar, distilled
1 cup	Guava Nectar, canned
1 cup	Tamarind Nectar, canned
1 cup	Papaya/Pineapple Nectar, canned
1 cup	Brown Sugar, golden Brown
1/4 cup	Molasses
4 ounces	Soy Sauce, lite

Combine all the above ingredients together in a sauce pot and blend well.

3 TB.	Dry Mustard, Coleman's
2 ounces	Grain Mustard, stone ground
1 TB.	Garlic Powder
1 TB.	Chili Powder
2 tsp.	Black Pepper, table grind
2 tsp.	Red Pepper, crushed
2 ounces	Worcestershire Sauce

Combine all the dry ingredients, mustard and Worcestershire together to form a smooth paste. Add the spice paste to the liquid and stir in well. Place on the heat and bring to a boil. Reduce the heat and simmer until the sauce is thickened (able to coat the back of a ladle). Reduce about 1/3 way down about one hour. Remove from the heat and store until needed.

Makes: about 2 quarts.

Note: Nectars can be found in most grocery stores in the Hispanic food aisle.

TERIYAKI BBQ SAUCE

My favorite Hawaiian Style Sauce for Chicken and Shrimp.

3 cups	Tomato Puree, canned
1 1/2 cups	Pineapple Juice, fresh
1 1/2 cups	Soy Sauce, low sodium
2 cups	Rice Wine Vinegar
1/2 tsp.	Ginger, ground
1 cup	Molasses, unsulphured
1/2 TB.	Caramel Color
1/2 pound	Brown Sugar, dark brown
1/2 TB.	Garlic Powder

Place all ingredients in a large sauce pot. Stir with whip to blend ingredients thoroughly, then place on the stove and bring to a full boil. As soon as the sauce boils, allow to simmer ONE MINUTE ONLY. Cool the sauce and place in a container for storage and refrigerate until needed.

Makes: about 2 1/2 quarts.

WHISKEY BBQ SAUCE

Sauce flavor improves with age, so make the sauce in advance!
Warm sauce for dipping or glazing.

4 ounces	White Onions, minced
1 TB.	Garlic, fresh, minced
3/4 cup	Whiskey
2 cups	Ketchup
3/4 cups	Molasses
1/2 cup	Corn Syrup, light
1/3 cup	White Vinegar
1/4 cup	Tomato Paste
1/4 cup	Worcestershire Sauce
1/2 tsp.	Lemon Pepper
1/2 tsp.	Kosher Salt
1/3 tsp.	Hot Sauce

Combine onion, garlic and whiskey in a sauce pan. Cook for about 3 minutes. Add the remaining ingredients, blend well. Place back on the stove and bring to a boil. Turn down the heat and simmer for 20 minutes, stirring constantly. Strain sauce to remove pieces of garlic and onion.

Makes: about 5 cups.

Brines & Cures

Brown Sugar Cure for Chicken
Brown Sugar Brine For Whole Turkey
Simple Brine for Poultry
Honey Brine for Chicken
Dry Cure for Smoked Salmon
Maple Brine for Turkey
OJ Brine for Poultry
Smoked Trout/Salmon Brine
Honey Maple Brine for Salmon
Sugar Cure for Shellfish

BROWN SUGAR CURE FOR CHICKEN

The use of the brown sugar cure will make your chicken look like it was sprayed with "Gold" after it is smoked! Makes for an outstanding smoked color.

1 cup	Brown Sugar, light
1 TB.	Garlic Salt
2 tsp.	Rib Stars Hot Rub (page 115)
2 tsp.	Seasoning Salt

Mix the dry ingredients together, blending well.

Notes: Makes enough cure for 6 whole chicken breast.

BROWN SUGAR BRINE FOR WHOLE TURKEY

This gives you a little Oriental BBQ Flavor to your smoked turkey.

3 quarts	Water
2 cups	Brown Sugar, light
1 1/2 cups	Soy Sauce, lite
1 cup	Maple Syrup
3/4 cup	Kosher Salt
6 each	Bay Leaf
3 TB.	Lemon Pepper
2 TB.	Garlic Powder
1 TB.	Ginger, ground
1 tsp.	Cloves, ground
1 tsp.	Chinese 5 Spice

Combine all the ingredients in a sauce pot, using only 1 quart of water. Bring to a boil. Simmer 5 minutes, then remove from the heat, add the last 2 quarts of cold water. Chill thoroughly before using the brine.

Enough brine for 14 pound turkey. Brine the turkey in a roasting bag for at least 12 hours and no more than 24 hours.

SIMPLE BRINE FOR POULTRY

You can add your own additional flavorings to this moisture enchancer!

1/2 cup	Kosher Salt
1/4 cup	Sugar
2 cups	Hot Tap Water
1 1/2 quarts	Cold Water

In the hot tap water, stir in the kosher salt and sugar. Let stand for 10 minutes to allow salt to dissolve. Add the cold water and stirring to mix.

Once brine is cooled down, submerge your poultry completely and refrigerate for the neccessary length of time.

HONEY BRINE FOR CHICKEN

For GREAT flavorful, moist chicken, this is my favorite!

1/2 cup	Kosher Salt
1/2 cup	Honey
1/4 cup	Garlic Juice
1/4 cup	Onion Juice
2 cups	Hot Tap Water
1 1/2 quarts	Cold Water

In the hot tap water, stir in the kosher salt, honey, garlic juice and onion juice, stir to dissolve and combine well. Let stand for 10 minutes for flavor to combine. Add the cold water and stir to mix.

Once brine is cooled down, submerge your chicken completely and refrigerate for the neccessary length of time.

DRY CURE FOR SMOKED SALMON

Use this cure for a low smoked salmon, brining is not needed when using this dry cure!

3 pounds	Kosher Salt
3 pounds	Sugar Superfine
3 pounds	Hickory Salt
2 pounds	Brown Sugar, light
1 pound	Brown Sugar, dark
1/3 cup	Coriander, dry
1/2 cup	Cumin
1/4 cup	Chili Powder
2 bunches	Cilantro, fresh

Mix all the ingredients together and store covered until needed.

Notes: Makes enough cure for 6 sides of salmon.

MAPLE BRINE FOR TURKEY

This one of my favorite brines for the holdiay season!

3 cups	Water
1 1/2 cups	Maple Syrup, real
1 TB.	Molasses
1 TB.	Lime Juice, fresh
1 TB.	Kosher Salt
1 TB.	Onion Juice
2 each	Bay Leaves
10 each	Peppercorns, whole
2 each	Garlic Cloves, minced
1 tsp.	Ginger, ground
2 tsp.	Mustard Seed, whole

Combine all the ingredients together and bring to a boil for 3 minutes. Remove for the heat and let cool down in a glass bowl.

Notes: Once cooled completely, add the whole turkey or breast, making sure that they are covered with the brine.

OJ BRINE FOR POULTRY

Something different for your poultry flavors. The vinegars in this brine add a nice little bite to the flavor.

1 gallon	Orange Juice
2 cups	Rice Wine Vinegar
2 cups	Raspberry Vinegar
1 cup	Brown Sugar, light brown
1 TB.	Garlic Juice
1 bunch	Cilantro, chopped
6 each	Star Anise
2 each	Cinnamon Stick, broken
2 TB.	Red Pepper Flakes
1 TB.	Whole Cloves
2 TB.	Black Peppercorns, whole
1 cup	Kosher Salt

Combine all the brine ingredients and place in a large stock pot. Bring the brine to a boil, reduce to low and simmer for 45 minutes. Let cool.

Notes: Makes enough brine for two 3 pound whole chickens.

SMOKED TROUT / SALMON BRINE

This is a sure fire simple brine for seafood.
Gives the seafood fillets a nice flavor.

1 quart	Water, hot
1/2 cup	Kosher Salt
1/2 cup	Brown Sugar, dark
2 TB.	Lemon Juice, fresh
1 TB.	Garlic Powder
1 TB.	Onion Powder

Carefully measure out the hot water and place it into a plastic container. Add the salt, juice and seasonings to the hot water and stir to completely dissolve.

COOL TO ROOM TEMPERATURE BEFORE USING TO MARINATE TROUT OR SALMON.

Notes: Makes enough brine for 10 fillets of trout or one side of salmon.

HONEY MAPLE BRINE FOR SALMON

This brine gives you an OUTSTANDING sweet smoked salmon.

2 quarts	Water, hot
1 cup	Kosher Salt
1 cup	Honey
1 cup	"Real" Maple Sryup
1/2 cup	Fresh Lemon Juice
2 TB.	Garlic Juice
1 TB.	Allspice
1 TB.	Cracked Black Pepper

Carefully measure out the hot water and place it into a plastic container. Add the salt, juice and seasonings to the hot water and stir to completely dissolve.

COOL TO ROOM TEMPERATURE BEFORE USING TO MARINATE TROUT OR SALMON.

Notes: Makes enough brine for two 3 pound sides of salmon. (Brine for 8 hours)

SUGAR CURE FOR SHELLFISH

Make your scallops look like "gold" nuggets with this sugar cure!

1 cup	Kosher Salt
1 cup	Sugar Superfine
3/4 cup	Brown Sugar, light
3/4 cup	Brown Sugar, dark
2 TB.	Galic Powder
2 TB.	Onion Powder

Mix all the ingredients together and store covered until needed. Cure seafood to be used for about 4-5 hours. Then rinse well and dry before smoking.

Notes: Enough cure for 3-4 pounds of scallops, shrimp or lobster tail meat.

Dry Rubs

Beef Rib Rub
"Rub Me Tender"™ Brisket Rub
Brisket Rub II
FGB Seasoning
Rib Stars® Hot Rib Rub
KC Dry Rub
Memphis Rib Rub
Pulled Pork Rub
Sparerib Rub
Backyard Chicken Rub

BEEF RIB RUB

Good strong rub to use on beef ribs, which need a nice salty flavorful rub!

1/2 cup	Kosher Salt
1/4 cup	Garlic Salt
1/2 cup	Black Pepper, table grind
1/2 cup	Paprika
1/4 cup	Chili Powder
2 TB.	Brown Sugar, dark
1/2 TB.	Sage, dry

Mix together all the ingredients and blend well. Store in an airtight container until needed.

Makes: 2 cups.

"RUB ME TENDER"™ BRISKET RUB

Very nice rub for brisket and making burnt ends!

1 cup	Turbinado Sugar
1/2 cup	Kosher Salt
1/4 cup	Garlic Salt
1/4 cup	Seasoning Salt
1/4 cup	Granulated Onion
1/4 cup	Chili Powder
1/4 cup	Brown Sugar
1/4 cup	Paprika
1/4 cup	Black Pepper
2 TB	Lemon Pepper
2 TB	Cayenne Pepper

Mix all ingredients together well. Sprinkle over both sides of the brisket.

BRISKET RUB II

Good heat in this rub, excellent for burnt ends!

3 TB.	Kosher Salt
3 TB.	Black Pepper, table grind
2 TB.	Paprika
1 1/2 TB.	Dry Mustard
1 TB.	Thyme, ground
1 TB.	Celery Seed, ground
1 TB.	Onion Powder
1 TB.	Garlic Powder
1/2 TB.	Cayenne Pepper
1 each	Bay Leaf, ground

Combine and mix all the ingredients well. Store in an airtight container until needed.

Makes about 1 cup.

FBG SEASONING

Excellent rub when smoking seafood!

1 TB.	Salt
1 TB.	Celery Salt
1 TB.	Dry Mustard
1 TB.	Paprika
1/2 TB.	Mace
1/4 tsp.	Ground Cloves
1/2 tsp.	Cinnamon
1/2 tsp.	Cayenne pepper
1/2 tsp.	Black Pepper, fine grind

Mix all ingredients together and blend well. Store in airtight container until needed.

Makes: 1/4 cup.

RIB STARS® HOT RIB RUB

Great Rub for Pork Ribs!

1 cup	Turbinado Sugar
1/2 cup	Kosher Salt
1/4 cup	Chili Powder
2 TB.	Granulated Onion
2 TB.	Granulated Garlic
2 TB.	Paprika
4 tsp.	Black Pepper, fine grind
4 tsp.	White Pepper, fine grind
3 tsp.	Oregano, ground
2 tsp.	Cayenne Pepper, ground
2 tsp.	Cumin, ground
2 tsp.	Allspice, ground

Combine all ingredients, blend well. Store in an airtight container until needed.

Note: Turbinado Sugar (Sugar in the raw)

Makes: 2 cups.

KC DRY RUB

Good all purpose rub for your backyard.

1 cup	Superfine Sugar
1/4 cup	Seasoning Salt
1/4 cup	Garlic Salt
1/4 cup	Celery Salt
1/4 cup	Onion Salt
1/2 cup	Paprika
3 TB.	Chili Powder, dark
2 TB.	Black Pepper, table grind
1 TB.	Lemon Pepper
2 tsp.	Sage, ground
1 tsp.	Dry Mustard
1/2 tsp.	Thyme, ground
1/2 tsp.	Cayenne pepper

Combine all ingredients together and store in an airtight container until needed.

Makes: 3 cups.

MEMPHIS RIB RUB

This rub gives ribs a nice flavor with basil and lower salt level.

1 cup	Superfine Sugar
2 TB.	Granulated Garlic
4 TB.	Onion Powder
3 TB.	Chili Powder
1 TB.	Lemon Pepper
2 TB.	Paprika
2 TB.	Kosher Salt
1 TB.	Seasoning Salt
1/2 TB.	Basil Leaves, dry

Combine all ingredients and blend well. Store in an airtight container until needed.

Makes: 2 cups.

PULLED PORK RUB

I have won numerous awards for my pulled pork, and this is the rub I use before smoking and pulling.

1/2 cup	Chili Powder, dark
1/4 cup	Paprika
1 TB.	Kosher Salt
1 TB.	Cumin, ground
1 TB.	Poultry Seasoning, ground
1 TB.	Superfine Sugar
1 TB.	Garlic Powder

Combine all ingredients and blend well. Store in an airtight container.

Notes: Don't be afraid to coat the pork butts fairly heavy on all sides. Because of the low salt ratio, I like to put this rub on 12 hours ahead. Get a nice thick bark when smoking before pulling the pork.

Makes: about 1 cup.

SPARERIB RUB

A milder rub than the hot rub for pork ribs.

4 TB.	Brown Sugar
2 TB.	Paprika
1 1/2 TB.	Seasoning Salt
1 1/2 TB.	Celery Salt
1 TB.	Black Pepper, table grind
1 TB.	Cayenne Pepper, ground
1 TB.	Onion Powder
1 1/2 tsp.	Chili Powder
1 tsp.	Cumin, ground

Combine all ingredients and blend well. Store in an airtight container and store until needed.

Makes: 3/4 cup.

BACKYARD CHICKEN RUB

The poultry seasoning in this rub matches very well with chicken and other poultry products.

1 cup	Sugar Turbinado
1/2 cup	Onion Salt
1/2 cup	Garlic Salt
1/2 cup	Paprika, sweet
2 TB.	Lemon Pepper
2 TB.	Chili Powder
2 TB.	Black Pepper, table grind
1 TB.	Poultry Seasoning
1 tsp.	Cumin, ground
1 tsp.	Cayenne, ground

Mix all ingredients together well. Sprinkle lightly over the chicken on all sides and under skin.

Makes: 3 cups.

Jerky Meats

Simple Beef Jerky
Spicy Beef Jerky
Sweet Chicken Jerky
Teriyaki Beef Jerky
Venison Jerky
Winter Turkey Jerky

SIMPLE BEEF JERKY

This recipe is simple and loaded with that traditional jerky flavor.

2 pounds	Round or Flank Steak
1/2 cup	Soy Sauce, lite
2 Tb.	Brown Sugar
1 tsp.	Liquid Smoke Flavoring
1 tsp.	Black Pepper, table grind

Combine all the dry ingredients with the liquids and blend well. Sliced the meat across the grain in thin slices (1/8") and marinade for 24 hours. Drain well and pat dry before cooking.

Place in a 190° smoker, flat on the meat grill. Make sure the meat is not touching. Smoke until done, at least 6 hours.

Meat should be dry and chewy.

Approximate Cooking Time: 6 hours

SPICY BEEF JERKY

If you looking to take it up a notch in the "heat" flavor, this is the jerky for you.

3 pounds	Round or Flank Steak
6 TB.	Worcestershire Sauce
4 TB.	A-1® Steak Sauce
2 TB.	Soy Sauce, lite
1 tsp.	Asian Chili Paste
3 each	Garlic gloves, crushed
2 tsp.	Kosher Salt
1/2 tsp.	Cayenne Pepper
1/2 tsp.	Lemon Pepper
2 tsp.	Onion Salt

Combine all the dry ingredients with the liquids and blend well. Sliced the meat across the grain in thin slices (1/8") and marinade for 24 hours. Drain well and pat dry before cooking.

Place in a 190° smoker, flat on the meat grill. Make sure the meat is not touching. Smoke until done, at least 6 hours.

Meat should be dry and chewy.

Approximate Cooking Time: 6 hours

SWEET CHICKEN JERKY

A nice change from eating beef jerky all the time!

3 pounds	Chicken Tenders, raw, flattened
1/2 cup	Soy Sauce, lite
8 TB.	Honey
6 each	Garlic Cloves, minced
1 TB.	Crushed Red Pepper Flakes
2 TB.	Black Pepper, table grind
1 1/2 TB.	Salad Oil

Combine the dry ingredients with the liquids. Marinade the flattened chicken tenders for 12 hours. Drain and pat dry before cooking. Smoke on flat rack in smoker for 4 hours at 190°, or until done.

I prefer to use chicken tenders, which I flattened with a meat hammer. Wrap the tenders in saran wrap before pounding. Don't over pound! Flatten to about 1/8" thick!

Approximate Cooking Time: 4-5 hours

TERIYAKI BEEF JERKY

This jerky has the flavor of the islands,
a fruity BBQ flavor.

3 pounds	Round or Flank Steak
1 cup	Teriyaki BBQ Sauce (pg. 100), cold

Slice the meat across the grain in thin slices (1/8") and marinade for 24 hours. Drain well, place in a 190° smoker flat on the meat grill. Make sure the meat is not touching. Smoke until done, at least 6 hours, meat should be dry and chewy. Not brittle!

Approximate Cooking Time: 6 hours

VENISON JERKY

A neat change for the winter deer hunter besides making smoked sausage. This is one of my favorites!

2 pounds	Venison Round
1/2 cup	Teriyaki Sauce, Kikoman's®
2 TB.	Brown Sugar
1 tsp.	Garlic Powder
1 tsp.	Black Pepper, cracked
1/4 tsp.	Juniper Berries, crushed

Combine all the dry ingredients with the liquids and blend well. Slice the meat across the grain in thin slices (1/8") and marinade for 24 hours. Drain well and pat dry before cooking, place in a 190° smoker, flat on the meat grill. Make sure the meat is not touching. Smoke until done, at least 6 hours.

Meat should be dry, and chewy.

Approximate Cooking Time: 6 hours

WINTER TURKEY JERKY

Great for the holidays!

3 pounds	Turkey Breast, skinless
4 TB.	Worcestershire sauce
1 TB.	Salad Oil
1 TB.	Kosher Salt
1 TB.	Brown Sugar
1 TB.	Black Pepper, cracked
1 tsp.	Garlic Powder
1/4 tsp.	Rubbed Sage

Combine all the dry ingredients with the liquids and blend well. Slice the meat across the grain in thin slices (1/8") and marinade for 24 hours. Drain well and pat dry before cooking, place in a 190° smoker, flat on the meat grill. Make sure the meat is not touching. Smoke until done, at least 6 hours.

Meat should be dry, and chewy.

Note: Freeze the breast slightly for easier slicing.

Approximate Cooking Time: 6 hours

Marinades/ Injections

10-2-4 Marinade for Pork Ribs
Award Winning Lamb Marinade
Bourbon Marinade for Pork Tenderloin
All Purpose Marinade
Orange Soy Hoisin Pork Marinade
Smoked Chicken Wing Marinade
Pink Pig Injection
Whiskey Turkey Injection
Whiskey Brisket Marinade
Honey Marinade for Lobster Tails
Coconut Curry Marinade for Scallops
Mustard Marinade for Shrimp

10-2-4 MARINADE FOR PORK RIBS

If you are a pepper freak like me, you will love the additional flavor!

2 cans	Dr. Pepper®
2 cups	Brown Sugar
1 cup	Pineapple Juice, canned
1 TB.	Worcestershire Sauce
4 cloves	Garlic, fresh, minced
2 TB.	Lemon Juice, fresh
1 tsp.	Sparerib Rub (page 118)
1 tsp.	Black Pepper, table grind

Combine all the ingredients. Marinate ribs for 24 hours.

Notes: Makes enough marinade for 3 slabs of ribs

AWARD WINNING LAMB MARINADE

I won my first Blue Ribbon with this marinade in the American Royal!

1 quart	Olive Oil
3 TB.	Rosemary, fresh
1 1/2 TB.	Oregano, dried
1 TB.	Black Pepper, coarse ground
1 pint	Lemon Juice, fresh
1 pint	Vermouth, dry
5 ounces	Garlic, fine minced
1 1/2 cups	Mint Leaves, fresh, chopped

Combine all the ingredients and blend well. Hold at room temperature for use in marinating and basting lamb.

Notes: Enough for one 5 pound leg of lamb.

BOURBON MARINADE FOR PORK TENDERLOIN

Give your Smoked Pork Tenderloin a new dimension in flavor with this one!

1/2 cup	Soy Sauce, Lite
1/2 cup	Bourbon
1/4 cup	Worcestershire Sauce
2 TB.	Brown Sugar
1/2 tsp.	Ginger, ground
1 TB.	Garlic, fresh, minced

Combine all the ingredients together, at least 12 hours before using.

Notes: Enough for two pork tenderloins.

ALL PURPOSE MARINADE

This makes a great All Purpose Marinade for poultry & pork!

2 cups	Salad Oil
1 cup	Dry Vermouth
1/4 cup	Lemon Juice, fresh
3 TB.	Lemon Pepper
1 TB.	Cracked Black Pepper
1 TB.	Kosher Salt
1 TB.	Fresh Garlic, minced
1/2 cup	Fresh Flat Parsley, minced

Combine all the ingredients together and blend well. Hold cold for use.

Note: Let marinade come to room temperature before using. Stir marinade to incorporate the ingredients again before using.

Use 1 cup of marinade per 2 pounds of meat.

ORANGE SOY HOISIN PORK MARINADE

This makes an awesome flavored Oriental Smoked Porkloin!

1/2 cup	Soy Sauce
1/2 cup	Orange Juice, fresh
4 TB.	Rice Wine Vinegar
2 TB.	Hoisin Sauce
2 TB.	Sesame Oil
2 TB.	Garlic, fresh minced
1 TB.	Brown Sugar
2 tesp.	Ginger, fresh, minced

Combine all ingredients and blend well.

Note: Use with pork tenderloin or porkloin. Place meat in a container and pour the marinade over the pork, marinade for at least 12 hours or overnight. Drain meat before smoking.

Enough for 2 pounds of meat.

SMOKED CHICKEN WING MARINADE

This is on of the Team's favorite recipes.
Developed by Chef Scott Allen

2 cups	Soy Sauce
2 cups	Teriyaki Sauce, Kikoman's®
4 ounces	Brown Sugar

Combine the ingredients together and pour over the chicken wings (1st & 2nd joints only). Marinade for 24 hours, turning several times to insure proper marinading. Drain the wings and place into the smoker at 200°. Smoke until wings are done and cooked to the bone, about 2 hours.

Notes: Enough for 5 pounds of wings.

PINK PIG INJECTION

Makes for a colorful pig roast!

1 cup	Vodka
2 cups	Cranberry Juice
1- 16 oz. can	Jellied Cranberry Sauce
1/2 cup	Olive Oil
4 TB.	Chili Powder
1 cup	Maraschino Cherry Juice
2 tsp.	Onion Juice
1/3 cup	Balsamic Vinegar
2 TB.	Dry Mustard
2 TB.	Paprika
1 tsp.	Basil
1/2 tsp.	Red Pepper, ground
1/3 cup	Soy Sauce
1/4 cup	Hoisin sauce
1 TB.	Celery Salt

Simmer together the day before injection. Day of, reheat and let cool completely before injecting into the whole hog. Inject the marinade into several places. Reserve some marinade for basting the hog.

Note: Enough for one 40-50 pound pig.

WHISKEY TURKEY INJECTION

The heat can be controlled by increasing or decreasing the Hot Chili Oil. Hot Chili Oil can be found in most oriental food markets.

1/2 cup	Honey
1/2 cup	Garlic Oil
1/2 cup	Butter, melted
1/4 cup	Kentucky Whiskey
1 tsp.	Cumin, ground
1 tsp.	Hot Chili Oil

Combine all ingredients together and blend well.

Note: This is enough injection for a 10-12 pound turkey.

WHISKEY BRISKET MARINADE

Change up your birsket flavor with a little bit of the Ole' South flavor.

1/2 cup	Brown Sugar, dark
1/3 cup	Whiskey
1/3 cup	Worcestershire Sauce
1/3 cup	Water
1 TB.	Soy Sauce
1 TB.	Black Pepper, table grind
1 TB.	Garlic Juice
1 TB.	Onion Juice

Combine whiskey with the remaining ingredients and mix well. Place the brisket in a large container or plastic bag. Cover with the whiskey marinade. Seal and refrigerate 12 hours, turning occasionally.

Notes: Enough for one 6-8 pound brisket flat.

HONEY MARINADE FOR LOBSTER TAILS

If you are into shellfish, this is a crowd pleaser!

2 cups	Seafood Stock or Borth
1 cup	Honey, 100% clover
1/2 cup	White Wine, dry
1 TB.	Peanut Oil
1 TB.	Kosher Salt
1 tsp.	Stone Ground Mustard
2 tsp.	Thyme, dried, ground

Combine all ingredients and bring to a boil. Cool completely before using.

Make seafood stock using the shells of the lobster tails. Use 4 shells from tails and bring to a boil in 3 cups of water. Simmer for 20 minutes than reduce until only two cups remain. Strain and cool for use.

Makes: Enough for the 4 lobster tails.

COCONUT CURRIED MARINADE FOR SCALLOPS

These scallops are as sweet as sugar and melt in your mouth!

2 TB.	Peanut Oil
1 cup	Coconut Milk, canned
4 TB.	Brown Sugar
2 cloves	Garlic, minced
2 tsp.	Curry Powder

Combine all ingredients and place the scallops in the marinade for 2 hours.

Makes: Enough for 1 pound of scallops.

MUSTARD MARINADE FOR SHRIMP

The mustard adds a unique flavor to these treasures for your taste buds!

1 1/2 cups	Salad Oil
1/2 cup	White Wine
1 TB.	Lemon Juice, fresh
3 TB.	Stone Ground Dijon Mustard
1 tsp.	Black Pepper, cracked
1 tsp.	Kosher Salt
1 tsp.	Fresh Dill, minced

Combine all the ingredients together and blend well. Hold cold for use. Stir marinade to incorporate the ingredients again, before using.

Note: 1 cup of marinade is needed per pound of shrimp. Marinate shrimp for 15-20 minutes. Shrimp will become tough if you marinate too long!

RIB STARS®

Meats:

Beef & Misc.

"Hell" Fire Brisket
Backyard Beef Ribs
Horseradish Brisket
"In Your Mouth" Brisket
Mustard & Pepper Spiced Beef Tenderloin
Venison Roast
Boneless Rack of Lamb
Garlic Leg of Lamb

"HELL" FIRE BRISKET

This one will sure jump start your tastebuds! (For additional flavor flat can be marinated in the Hell Fire Mop over night.) Drain and dry the brisket before applying the dry rub.

1 each	8-10lb. Brisket Flat trimmed, slightly
4 TB.	Rub Me Tender™ Rub (page 113)
2 cups	Hell Fire Mop (page 181), room temperature

Trim the brisket of any excess fat, down to about 1/4" thickness, the fat helps keep the brisket moist during cooking. Once the flat is trimmed. Place in a large zip lock bag and pour half of the mop over the brisket. Marinate brisket for at least 12 hours. Drain and pat dry before sprinkling each side of the brisket with an even layer of the brisket rub.

Place the brisket on a platter and set at room temperature, while your smoker comes to temp.

Bring the smoker to about 300°, place the brisket in the middle of the smoker, and smoke at 225°. I recommend smoking brisket flats at the rate of 1 hour for every pound. Start mopping the brisket after the first 2-3 hours, after the bark has formed. Mop the brisket every 1 1/2 to 2 hours until mop is used up or brisket is done. Cook brisket until the meat is tender. (Internal temp. 195°).

Notes: I only like to use the single muscle brisket flat, which is the bottom muscle of the brisket. For beginners, the single muscle is easy to deal with and easier to slice.

Special Note: Most briskets are tender when the internal temperature reaches 195°.

Approximate Cooking Time: 8-10 hours

Wood Suggestion: Pecan & Cherry

BACKYARD BEEF RIBS

If you haven't tried beef ribs, you'll need to add this one to your files!

2 slabs	Beef Ribs, skinned
1/2 cup	Rub Me Tender™ Rub
1 batch	Backyard BBQ Mop (page 184), warm
1 cup	Brown Sugar

Remove the membrane from the back side of the ribs. Trim any excess fat and sprinkle both sides with the rub, using more of the rub on the meat side of the ribs. Allow the ribs to sit for at least 4 hours in the refrigerator.

While the smoker is heating to temperature, pull the beef ribs out of the refrigerator and let sit at room temperature for 1 hour or until the smoker is ready to go.

Once the smoker is preheated, place the rubbed ribs into the smoker and smoke at 250°. Smoke the ribs for three hours and than start mopping with Backyard BBQ Mop.

After 4 hours remove the ribs and place on a sheet of foil. Sprinkle the top of the ribs evenly with brown sugar. Pour about 1/2 cup of the remaining mop over the ribs and seal in the foil. Place them back in the smoker and smoke for another 2 hours, checking them after the first hour to see if they are bone tender.

Once the ribs are tender remove them from the foil and place back in the smoker, finish brush with the remaining mop. Cook for about 30 to 45 minutes longer and remove from the smoker.

The brown sugar will give them a nice gooey and sweet coating. The mixture of the mop and sugar makes a nice sauce on the ribs before they are done.

Approximate Cooking Time: 6-8 hours

Wood Suggestion: Sugar Maple

HORSERADISH BRISKET

Wake up your taste buds with this zipped up flavor on the outside of your brisket!

1 each	8-10lbs. Brisket Flat, trimmed slightly
2 TB.	Pourable Yellow Mustard
1 cup	Rub Me Tender™ Brisket Rub (page 113)
2 1/2 cups	H & M Brisket Mop (page 185)
1/4 cup	Horseradish, prepared

Trim the brisket flat of any excess fat, leaving about 1/4" fat trim. Do not remove all of the fat since the fat helps keep the brisket moist. Once the fat is trimmed, spread a tablespoon of mustard on each side of the brisket. Sprinkle each side of the brisket with an even layer of the Brisket Rub. Place the brisket on a platter and set at room temperature while your smoker comes to temperature.

Preheat the smoker to about 300 degrees. Reduce the temperature to 225° and place the brisket in the smoker. Smoke at 225° for 3 hours. Once the brisket has smoked for three hours and formed the bark, start to mop with the H & M Mop. Mop the brisket every 1 1/2 to 2 hours.

About two hours before the brisket is done place in foil. Before closing the foil, spread the horseradish on top of the Brisket. Wrap tight and finish cooking. When brisket reaches 195° internal temperature remove from the smoker, open the foil slightly on the top and allow the brisket to cool down before slicing.

Special Note: Most briskets are tender when the internal temperature reaches 195°.

Approximate Cooking Time: 8-10 hours

Wood Suggestion: Mulberry & Cherry

"IN YOUR MOUTH" BRISKET

This is one of our favorite ways of doing brisket!

1 each	8-10lbs. Brisket, trimmed slightly
1 cup	Brisket Rub II (page 114)
1 cup	Spiced Brisket Mop (page 190)
1/2 cup	Double "J" BBQ Sauce (page 94)

Trim the brisket of any excess fat. Do not remove all of the fat since the it helps keep the brisket moist during cooking. Once the fat is trimmed, place brisket in a large zip lock bag. Pour one batch of Brisket Mop over the brisket and marinate for 6 hours! Remove and pat dry before putting on the brisket rub. Rub well on both sides with the Dry Rub. Place the brisket on a platter and set at room temperature, while your smoker comes to temperature.

Bring the smoker to about 300 degrees. Place the brisket in the smoker, and smoke at 225° for 3 hours. Once the brisket has smoked for three hours and formed the bark, start to mop with the Spiced Brisket Mop. Mop the brisket every hour. Cook brisket until the internal temperature is 165°. Wrap in foil and continue cooking until the internal temperature reaches 195°.

Special Note: Most briskets are tender when the internal temperature reaches 195°.

Approximate Cooking Time: 8-10 hours

Wood Suggestion: Pecan & Cherry

MUSTARD & PEPPER SPICED BEEF TENDERLOIN

This is a sure winner on the beef side of cooking!

5 pound	Beef Tenderloin, whole, fully trimmed
1/2 cup	Dijon Stone Ground Mustard
2 TB.	Garlic Salt
2 TB.	Onion Salt
2 TB.	Black Pepper, table grind
1 TB.	Chili Powder
1 tsp.	Cayenne Pepper
1 tsp.	Cumin, ground

Trim the tenderloin of all fat and silver skin tissue and remove the side strap. After trimming the tenderloin, cut off 3" from the flat tail end, reserving the tail meat for other uses like grilling beef kabobs.

Combine all the spices together and form a dry rub. Rub the mustard over the whole surface of the tenderloin, covering all sides. Sprinkle the dry rub over all sides of the tenderloin and allow the tenderloin to sit at room temperature while the smoker is preheating.

Preheat the smoker. Once the smoker is preheated, run the temperature of the smoker at 225°.

Note: When the tenderloin reaches 145° internal temperature, remove it from the smoker and allow it to rest for 15-30 minutes before slicing.

Approximate Cooking Time: 2-3 hours

Wood Suggestion: Maple

VENISON ROAST

A little change during the fall season!

1 each	4-5 lbs. Venison Roast, trimmed
5 TB.	Brown Sugar
1 TB.	Black Pepper, table grind
1 tsp.	Sumac, ground
1 tsp.	Paprika
1/4 tsp.	Cayenne Pepper, ground

Trim the round, and combine the spices, mixing well. Rub the venison with the rub on all sides.

Place into the smoker at 225°. Plan on 40 minutes a pound. Wrap in foil about an hour before done. Allow roast to cool down with smoker while wrapped in the foil. This will also produce a nice au jus in the foil. That can be poured over the venison after it is sliced.

Notes: Rosemary twigs add a nice flavor to this meat while smoking.

Note: Ground Sumac can be found in specialty stores that carry Middle Eastern foods and spices.

Approximate Cooking Time: 5-6 hours

Wood Suggestion: Maple & Cherry

BONELESS RACK OF LAMB

The tenderness of this product is second only to the flavor-smoked meat!

4 each	Lamb Racks, boned from the rack and trimmed
1 cup	Lamb Marinade (page 129), cold

Remove the top layer of fat off the meat side of the lamb rack itself. Being very careful not to lose any meat, bone the eye of the muscle completely away from the rack of bones itself.

Trim the loin of lamb on both sides of any fat or grizzle. Place the loins in a pan and cover with the marinade, coating all sides of the lamb. Marinade for at least 12 hours, but not more than 24 hours. Remove from the marinade after 24 hours.

While the smoker is preheating to 225°, drain the lamb loins and allow the loins to sit at room temperature until the smoker is ready. Place the lamb in the smoker.

Notes: Reserve some of the marinade to baste the lamb with during the smoking process.

Approximate Cooking Time: 2 hours

Wood Suggestion: Sugar Maple & Apple (Branches of Rosemary)

GARLIC LEG OF LAMB

Try this one out at Easter time!

1 each	Leg of lamb, boneless, 4-5 lbs.
2 cup	Garlic, peeled
1 cup	Fresh Mint
1/2 cup	Fresh Rosemary Leaves
2 TB.	Black Pepper
2 TB.	Fresh Oregano
1 cup	Olive Oil

Combine all the ingredients, except the lamb, in a food processor and puree until smooth and thick.

Bone the leg of lamb or have your butcher bone and butterfly it for you. Once butterflied, layout flat on the cutting board. Rub the inside with half of the garlic puree. Roll the leg back together and tie with butcher twine to form a even diameter roll for smoking. Tie twine at even spaces about 2 inches apart. Rub the outside of the lamb with the remaining puree. Refrigerate and flavor for at least 8 hours or overnight.

Preheat the smoker. While smoker is preheating, remove the leg of lamb for the refrigerator. Drain off excess marinade. Allow the leg to sit at room temperature until the smoker is ready. Place in a smoker that is 225° and smoke until internal temperature of 145° is achieved.

Approximate Cooking Time: 4-5 hours
(you will want the leg to be medium when done)

Wood Suggestion: Sugar Maple & Apple
(Branches of Rosemary)

Meats:

Pork

"Pinky's" Pig Roast
Backyard Baby Back Ribs
Dr. Pepper® Spare Ribs
Rib Stars® "Take Your Breath Away" Ribs
Spiced Apple Cider Baby Back Ribs
Sweet & Spicy Cherry Ribs
Mustard Spare Ribs
Oriental Porkloin
Honey Bourbon Pork Tenderloin
Italian Sausage
Twice Smoked Pulled Pork

"PINKY'S" PIG ROAST

Great for a Luau, very interesting color from the cranberry juice.

1 each	45 lbs. Whole Pig, dressed
1 batch	Whole Pink Pig Injection (pg. 132), cold

Inject the pig 24 hours before smoking. Make sure injection is injected as deep to the bone as possible. Smoke the pig in a smoker at 250°, basting every hour after the first 2 hours with the remaining Pink Pig Injection.

When the ears, snout and tail begin to brown, cover them with foil.

Notes: Take the pig out of the smoker or from the heat when it reaches an internal temperature of 155°. Let it set for about 20 minutes before carving. If you are cooking with an offset smoker (firebox to the side) put the butt end closest to the fire hole.

If you are directly cooking over coals, place most of the heat source at the location of the shoulders and butt end.

At 225° allow about 15 minutes per pound for the pig to be done. Always use a meat thermometer to test for doneness. Pig is done when thermometer reaches 155° internal at the thickest part of the ham.

Approximate Cooking Time: 10-12 hours

Wood Suggestion: Apple & Cherry

BACKYARD BABY BACK RIBS

This recipe is an easy one for the new beginner, you can't go wrong on this one. The mop adds a nice sweetness to the rib.

3 slabs	Baby Back Ribs, prepared
6 TB.	KC Dry Rub (page 116)
2 cups	Basic Rib Mop (page 188)

Remove the membrane from the back side of the ribs. Place on a cutting board and sprinkle each side of the ribs with the rib rub. Wrap the ribs in saran wrap and refrigerate for about 4 hours. Allow them to sit at room temperature while your smoker is coming up to temperature.

Place the ribs in the smoker when the smoker reaches 250°. Smoke the ribs for 2 hours to form a rub crust before sopping. Allow the smoker to cool down to 225° and hold this temperature until done. Mop the ribs with the Standard Rib Mop every 15 minutes.

Notes: You can finish the ribs with your favorite sauce the last 30 minutes of the cooking time, this will allow plenty of time for the sauce to glaze without burning.

Approximate Cooking Time: 4-5 hours

Wood Suggestion: Maple & Cherry

DR PEPPER® SPARE RIBS

If you are a Pepper freak, like I am, you will love these unique flavored ribs!

3 slabs	Spare Ribs, skinned
1 batch	10-2-4 Marinade for Ribs (page 129)
6 TB.	Spare Rib Rub (page 118)

Reserve some of the marinade for mopping the ribs during the smoking process. Use the rest of the mop and marinate the ribs for 12 hours. Remove from marinade and pat dry. Sprinkle with rib rub on both sides. Allow the ribs to sit at room temperature until smoker is ready. Place rubbed ribs in smoker and smoke at 250°. Mopping every hour after the first two hours of smoking.

After two hours reduce the temperature to 225° until done.

Notes: Ribs can be basted with favorite sauce about 30 minutes before they are done. I prefer my ribs dry, and use sauced only for sopping at the table.

Approximate Cooking Time: 5-6 hours

Wood Suggestion: Sassafras & Cherry

RIB STARS® "TAKE MY BREATH AWAY" RIBS

Looking to Breathe some life into your ribs, then this is the recipe for you. Watch it! It may take your breath away!!

3 Slabs	Spareribs, special trimmed
6 TB.	Rib Stars® Hot Rub (page 115)
1 cup	"Take My Breath Away" Mop (page 186), room temperature
3/4 cup	"Take My Breath Away" BBQ Sauce, (page 97), room temperature

Remove the membrane from the back of the ribs. Trim away the flap meat from the back side of the ribs and cut through the sternum bone, removing this breast bone from the ribs completely. Paint each slab of ribs with the mop and marinade for two hours.

Sprinkle each side of the ribs with the rib rub and place the ribs in the 250° smoker.

Allow ribs to smoke for 5-6 hours and meat starts to pull away from the bones. Mop ribs with mop about every two hours. 30 minutes before serving ribs, brush both sides of the ribs with the Hawg's Breath BBQ Sauce.

Notes: Smoke the flap meat and the breast bone section along with the ribs. These are great for use in your baked bean recipe.

Approximate Cooking Time: 5-6 hours

Wood Suggestion: Sassafras & Cherry

SPICED APPLE CIDER BABY BACK RIBS

Using your mop as a marinade is another way of adding additional flavor to your smoke ribs.

3 slabs	Baby Back Ribs, peeled
1 batch	Apple Cider Rib Mop (page 183)
6 TB.	Rib Stars® Hot Rub (page 115)
3/4 cup	Honey
3/4 cup	"Take My Breath Away" BBQ Sauce, (page 97)

After peeling and preparing the ribs, marinate the ribs for 6 hours in the Apple Cider Rib Mop. Reserving some of the mop for the smoking process. Remove from marinade and pat dry. Sprinkle with rib rub on both sides, putting less on the bone side of the ribs. Let ribs stay at room temperature until smoker is ready. Place rubbed ribs in smoker and smoke at 250° . Mopping every hour after the first two hours of smoking.

After two hours allow smoker to reduce down in temperature to 225°. Hold this temperature until ribs are done.

Notes: Ribs can be basted with favorite sauce about 15-20 minutes before they are done.

Approximate Cooking Time: 4-5 hours

Wood Suggestion: Apple & Cherry

SWEET & SPICY CHERRY RIBS

The Sorghum and the Chili Asian Paste gives these ribs a nice multilayered flavor! Just enough hot, and a little bit of sweet!

3 slabs	Baby Back Ribs, peeled
1 batch	Cherry Rib Mop (page 184)
6 TB.	KC Dry Rub (page 116)
3/4 cup	Honey, warm
3/4 cup	Rib Stars® Double "J" Sauce (page 94), room temperature

After peeling and preparing the ribs, marinate the ribs for 6 hours in the Cherry Rib Mop. Reserving some of the mop for the smoking process. Remove from marinade and pat dry. Sprinkle with rib rub on both sides, putting less on the bone side of the ribs. Let ribs stay at room temperature until smoker is ready. Place rubbed ribs in smoker and smoke at 250° . Mopping every hour after the first two hours of smoking.

After two hours allow smoker to reduce down in temperature to 225°, hold this temperature until ribs are done.

Notes: Brush the ribs with warm honey on both sides and then brush lightly with the double " J" Sauce. Place the ribs back in the smoker 20-30 minutes to allow the sauce to glaze the ribs.

Approximate Cooking Time: 4-5 hours

Wood Suggestion: Cherry & Maple

MUSTARD SPARERIBS

I love doing spareribs , because I love their excellent pork flavor. The little kick of mustard in this recipe, kicks up the final flavor!

3 slabs	Spareribs, trimmed & skinned
3/4 cup	Mustard, yellow pourable
3/4 cups	Spare Rib Rub (pg. 118)
1 batch	Mustard Spare Rib Mop (pg. 185)

Trim your spare ribs of any excess fat or meat. You can also trim the spares down to St. Louis style, by removing the skirt meat and breast bone.

While the smoker is reaching temperature, spread the spare ribs on both sides with the yellow mustard. Sprinkle the dry rub to both sides of the ribs.

Place the ribs in the smoker at 250°. Cook ribs until tender, about 5-6 hours. I prefer to use a spray bottle when I use this mop. (Strain the mop first before using a spray bottle.)

Approximate Cooking Time: 5-6 hours

Wood Suggestion: Sassafras & Cherry

ORIENTAL PORKLOIN

This recipe is one of my favorites for changing up the pace on producing unique flavors out of your smoker.

1 each	Whole 3 lb. Porkloin, trimmed, boneless
1 batch	Orange Soy Hoisin Marinade (page 131) cold, prepared

Place the porkloins in a shallow dish and cover with the marinade. Marinate for at least 12 hours. Remove the pork and drain well. Let the meat sit for 30 minutes while your smoker reaches 225°. Place the porkloins in the smoker and smoke until an internal temperature of 155°.

Approximate Cooking Time: 2 hours

Wood Suggestion: Pecan or Maple

HONEY BOURBON PORK TENDERLOIN

Another outstanding change of flavor for your pork tastebuds!

1 cup	Olive oil
1/4 cup	Honey
1/4 cup	Bourbon
1/2 cup	Orange Juice
1 TB.	Garlic, minced
1/4 cup	Soy Sauce, lite
1 TB.	Stone Ground Mustard
2 TB.	Sage, fresh, chopped
2 tsp.	Lemon Pepper
1 tsp.	Kosher Salt

Combine all ingredients together, blend well. Place the pork tenders in a glass dish and pour the marinade over the meat. Marinade covered for 12 hours. Turning tenders several times. Drain and pat pork dry before cooking. Place in 225° smoker and smoke until 155° internal temperature.

Approximate Cooking Time: 2 hours

Wood Suggestion: Apple

ITALIAN SAUSAGE

There isn't anything like making your own sausage. I like to just wrap my bulk sausage in saran wrap, chill well, unwrap and then smoke! No casings needed!

4 pounds	Pork Butts, boneless
1/4 cup	Tomato Paste
1/2 cup	Parsley, fresh, minced
4 ounces	Provolone cheese, grated
5 ounces	Romano cheese, grated
1 TB.	Fresh Garlic, minced
1 TB.	Fennel Seeds, crushed
1 TB.	Oregano, dry
1 TB.	Black Pepper, fine grind
2 tsp.	Kosher Salt
2 tsp.	Garlic Powder
2 tsp.	Basil Leaves, dry
1 1/2 tsp.	Sage, dry
1 tsp.	Crushed Red Pepper, flakes

Cut the pork into large cubes, combine with the paste, parsley and provolone cheese. Using plastic gloves, toss the ingredients together, blending well and keeping cold!

Combine all the dry seasonings, garlic and cheeses together in a small bowl. Sprinkle over the meat and mix in to blend. Using plastic gloves, mix by hand to evenly distribute the meat and seasonings.

Place a 1/4" grind plate in the grinder and grind meat into a well chilled bowl. Keep all ingredients well chilled.

Use sausage in bulk form or place into casings making 4 ounce links.

Notes: Place the food grinder & attachments in a container of ice water to thoroughly chill before preparation of the ingredients.

TWICE SMOKED PULLED PORK

I have won numerous ribbons and awards for my twice smoked pulled pork. You can't go wrong with this winner!

4 pounds	Boston Butt, bone-in, trimmed
4 TB.	Pulled Pork Rub (page 117)
1 cup	Brown Sugar, golden brown
2 cup	Pulled Pork Mop (page 188), warmed

*****Finishing Flavors*****

1/2 cup	"Take Your Breath Away" Sauce (pg. 97), warmed
1/4 cup	Maple Syrup, "real"
1/4 cup	Pulled Pork Mop (page 188), warmed
1/4 cup	Brown Sugar
1 TB.	Pulled Pork Rub (page 117),
1 TB.	Hot Sauce

Sprinkle dry rub on all surfaces of the butt, and rub into meat. Cover and store in refrigerator for 12 hours. Get smoker temperature up to 300°. Place butt into smoker and layer the top of each pork butt with 1 cup of brown sugar. Set the smoker temperature to 210°. Smoke for 3 hours before starting to baste butts to ensure a nice crust on the outer edges. Hold temperature at 210° and smoke butts for 6 hours. Basting with pulled pork mop every hour after the first 3 hours! When the pork reaches 165°, wrap the butts in double strength foil with some of the pulled pork mop. Continue to cook meat for another 4 hours or until they are ready to fall apart. Remove from the smoker, allow the meat to cool (in the foil), once cooled, hand pull. Allow meat to stay in large pulled chunks. Add the finishing flavors. Do not mix into the meat at this point. Place the pan back into smoker about 1 hour before service to increase the smoke flavor. Just before service toss the meat well.

Approximate Cooking Time: 9-10 hours

Wood Suggestion: Sugar Maple or Pecan & Cherry

RIB STARS®

Meats:

Poultry

Brown Sugar Maple Cured Chicken Breast
Duck Pastrami
OJ Cornish Hens
Whiskey Turkey Breast
Brown Sugar Brined Whole Turkey
Holiday Maple Brined Turkey
Smokin' Good Chicken
Passion Chicken Thighs
Soy Brown Sugar Wings

BROWN SUGAR MAPLE CURED CHICKEN BREAST

The color on this smoked chicken is awesome and the chicken breast are loaded with moisture.

6 each	8 oz. Chicken Breast, bone in split
1/2 cup	Fresh Apple Cider or Pineapple Juice
1/4 cup	Maple Syrup, "real"
1 TB.	Onion Juice
1 TB.	Garlic Juice
1 cup	Brown Sugar Cure (page 105)

Trim bone-in chicken of any excessive fat, leaving the skin on. Wash chicken well and pat dry. Place the chicken in a plastic ziplock bag. Combine all the ingredients together, except the brown sugar cure. Sprinkle the brown sugar cure over the chicken in the zip lock bag and work into both sides of the chicken. Pour the liquid mixture into the bag and make sure the chicken is coated on both sides. Cure for 8 hours.

Approximate Cooking Time: 2 hours

Wood Suggestion: Apple

DUCK PASTRAMI

If you like duck, you will love this cured and smoked product. Give you sandwich a change with this pastrami.

2 pounds	Duck Breast, skinned
1 TB.	Tri-Color Peppercorns, cracked
2 tsp.	Thyme, dry
2 each	Bay Leaves, crushed
1 tsp.	Whole Cloves
2 TB.	Fresh Garlic, minced
2 tsp.	Juniper Berries, crushed
1/4 tsp.	Dry Sage, rubbed
4 cups	Water
1/2 cup	Brown Sugar, light
1/4 cup	Kosher Salt
1/4 cup	Coarse Ground Pepper

In a mixing bowl, combine the peppercorns , thyme, bay leaves, cloves, garlic, sage and one teaspoon of the juniper berries. In a sauce pan bring the water, sugar and salt to a boil, stirring to dissolve. Remove from heat and add the dry spices and allow to steep for at least 1 hour. Place the duck breast in a bowl or plastic tub and pour the seasoned brine to cover the breast completely. Cover and refrigerate for 48 hours, turning the breast if needed. Before smoking remove the breast and pat dry, combine the remaining crushed berries and ground black pepper, then press the mixture into both sides of the duck breast.

Place the breasts in a 210° smoker and smoke for about 1 1/2 - 2 hours, until done!

Approximate Cooking Time: 1 1/2 - 2 hours

Wood Suggestion: Maple or Pecan

OJ CORNISH HENS

If you like smoking Cornish hens, these will become a favorite in your recipes.

8 each	Cornish game hens, split in half
1 batch	OJ Brine for Poultry (page 108), cold

Thoroughly rinse and dry the hens, inside and out. Place the hens in a large container and cover with the brine, make sure they are completely submerged. If container is not big enough to submerge them, you will need to turn it every 8 hours. Brine the hens for 24 hours under refrigeration. (Reserve some brine for mopping.)

Remove the hens from the brine, rinse off and pat dry.

Place the hens, skin side up, in the smoker at 225°. Use reserved brine to mop hens while smoking.

Approximate Cooking Time: 2 hours

Wood Suggestion: Apple or Cherry wood

WHISKEY TURKEY BREAST

Great tasting turkey breast at holiday time or anytime of the season.

1 each	10-12 lbs. Turkey Breast, bone-in
2 batches	Whiskey Turkey Injection (pg 132), room temperature

Place the turkey breast into a clear oven bag. Pour half of the injection liquid over the turkey breast and remove the air from the bag by twisting and then sealing the bag.

Allow the breast to brined for 24 hours. Rinse the turkey. Using the remaining half of the injection, pierce the turkey with a injection needle in several different spots. Inject the turkey with half of the injection. Place in smoker at 275°. Smoke until internal temperature of 165°.

Note: Spray with fruit juice or nectars during smoking, to keep skin moist.

Approximate Cooking Time: 4 hours

Wood Suggestion: Pecan with Cherry wood

BROWN SUGAR BRINED WHOLE TURKEY

This brown sugar turkey, is nice and moist with a slight flavor of soy and a touch of sweetness from the brown sugar and maple syrup.

1 each	12-14 lbs. Whole Turkey, fresh
1 batch	Brown Sugar Turkey Brine (page 105)

Brine the turkey for 24 hours, turning to ensure that the whole turkey gets brine on it. After brining, remove and pat dry and allow the turkey to air dry for 12 hours under refrigeration.

Heat your smoker to 300° and add the turkey to the smoker. Smoking the turkey at a higher temperature will allow the skin to render and stay moist and tender.

Note: Reserve some of the brine for basting the turkey during the smoking process. Do not use brine that has had the turkey in it. Use only a clean brine for basting.

Some brine can be reserved for injecting deep into the breast and thighs of the turkey before smoking.

I find it best to add some type of liquid to the smoker to aid in keeping the turkey moist.

Approximate Cooking Time: 4-5 hours

Wood Suggestion: Pecan with Cherry Wood

HOLIDAY MAPLE BRINED TURKEY

This brine gives you a nice deep brown color to your smoked turkey. Creating an oven roast look to the turkey.

1 each	12-14 lbs. Whole Turkey, fresh
2 batches	Maple Brine for Turkey (page 107)

Brine the turkey for 24 hours, turning to ensure that the whole turkey gets brine on it. After brining, remove and pat dry and allow the turkey to air dry for 12 hours under refrigeration.

Heat your smoker to 300° and add the turkey to the smoker. Smoking the turkey at a higher temperature will allow the skin to render and stay moist and tender.

Note: Reserve some of the brine for basting the turkey during the smoking process. Do not use brine that has had the turkey in it. Use only a clean brine for basting.

Some brine can also be injected deep into the breast and thighs of the turkey before smoking.

I find it best to add a some type of liquid to the smoker to aid in keeping the turkey moist.

Approximate Cooking Time: 4-5 hours

Wood Suggestion: Maple with Cherry Wood

SMOKIN' GOOD CHICKEN

This used to be a favorite on the barbecue circuit, using Italian Dressing and a good hearty rub!

1 each	3 lbs. Whole Chicken, cut into 8 pieces
2 cups	Italian Dressing, "Wishbone®"
as needed	Backyard Chicken Rub (pg 118)

Wash the 8 cut chicken well in lemon water. Rinse well. Trim the pieces of any excess fat. Place in a heavy container or large zip bags and pour the dressing over the chicken. Make sure all pieces are coated well. Close the bag and marinade for 4 hours in the refrigerator. After marinating, remove from the dressing and drain well.

Sprinkle the chicken lightly with Backyard Chicken Rub.

Place in the smoker, skin side up, at 300-350° for 2 hours. Halfway through the smoking process, turn the pieces of chicken over and finish cooking. This will allow the skin to stay tender. Cook until the juices run clear or the thighs are 165° internal temperature.

Approximate Cooking Time: 2 - 2 1/2 hours

Wood Suggestion: Apple or Cherry Wood

PASSION CHICKEN THIGHS

These plump thighs are loaded with flavor and juices the sauce adds the extra taste to your chicken taste buds!

12 each	Chicken Thighs, skin on, bone-in
1/2 cup	Backyard Chicken Rub (pg. 118)
as needed	Pineapple Juice
1 cup	Passion BBQ Sauce (pg. 99)

Wash the chicken thighs well in some lemon water and then rinse well. Trim the pieces of any excess fat. Sprinkle the chicken lightly with Backyard Chicken Rub. Sprinkle the bone side, skin side and a little rub under the skin (just loosen the skin on one end, do not completely remove). Allow the thighs to sit (under refrigeration) for 2 hours.

Place in the smoker, skin side up, at 300-350° for 2 hours. Halfway through the smoking process, turn the pieces of chicken over and finish cooking. This will allow the skin to stay tender. Cook until the juices run clear or the thighs are 165° internal temperature. Start spray mopping the thighs after you turn them over. Make sure to spray just before brushing with the passion sauce. Brush the sauce on after the thighs are done and return to the smoker for another 20-30 minutes to glaze the sauce.

Approximate Cooking Time: 1 1/2 - 2 hours

Wood Suggestion: Apple or Cherry Wood

SOY BROWN SUGAR WINGS

Outstanding different flavor for your wing fans. Try dipping these in the Spicy Three Mustard sauce!

5 pounds	Chicken Wings (split into drumettes & 2nd joints)
1 batch	Smoked Chicken Wing Marinade (pg 131)

Spicy Three Mustard Dipping Sauce

1 TB.	Dry Mustard Powder
1/2 cup	Pommery Mustard (stone ground)
1/2 cup	Dijon Mustard
1 ounce	White Wine, dry
1 TB.	Lemon Juice, fresh

Wash the chicken wings well in some lemon water and then rinse well. Trim the pieces of any excess fat. Place the wings in a plastic or glass bowl and pour the marinade over the wings. Marinate for 24 hours, turning the wings to ensure proper marinating on all sides. After marinating, drain well.

Place in the smoker at 250-275° for 2 hours. Halfway through the smoking process, turn the pieces of chicken over and finish cooking. This will allow the skin to stay tender.

Remove from the smoker and serve with the dipping sauce.

Note: When making the sauce, dissolve the dry mustard into the wine and lemon juice and stir well. This will keep the dry mustard from lumping up in the sauce. Add the mustards to the liquid mixture and stir well. Serve the dipping sauce cold.

Approximate Cooking Time: 1.5 - 2 hours

Wood Suggestion: White Oak & Cherry

Meats:

Seafood

Smoked Trout
Herbed Cured Salmon
Honey Marinated Lobster Tails
Coconut Curried Scallops
Mustard Marinated Shrimp
BBQ Spiced Catfish
Honey Maple Salmon

SMOKED TROUT

I like using boneless butterflied trout fillets. Smoke the fillets until just done. They are thin and cook at a faster pace!

10 each	Trout Fillets, boned
1 batch	Smoked Trout Brine (page 109, cold

Place the boneless fillets with the skin on, into the brine with skin side up. Marinate in the brine for 8 hours only.

After marinating, remove from the brine and pat dry with a clean cloth or towel. Air dry the fillets for one hour under refrigeration. And place on the racks in the smoker skin side down at 200°. Smoke until just done.

Notes: Can be used with Trout, Salmon and Catfish.

Try using different seasonings for added flavor. Add the seasoning after you have placed the fillets on your smoker rack.

Approximate Cooking Time: 30-45 minutes

Wood Suggestion: Oak or Maple

HERBED CURED SALMON

The herb in this recipe can be changed. Try using dill or an assortment of herbs for different flavors.

2 each	3-5 lbs. Salmon Sides, skin on, boneless
2 bunches	Cilantro, fresh
2 cups	Dry Cure for Smoked Salmon (page 107), prepared

Clean salmon fillets well and remove all pin bones. Using a perforated pan, make a bed with some of the fresh cilantro. Rub the skin side of the salmon with the dry cure and place skin side down. Rub the meat side with more rub and cover with more cilantro.

Rub second fillet with rub on the meat side and place on top of the first fillet, meat side to meat side. Cover with remaining cilantro. Top with double folded saran wrap, and place another perforated pan on top of the wrapped salmon. Weigh the pans down with bricks or cans. Place the pan in a deep pan to catch draining liquid. Store under refrigeration for 48 hours.

Remove and rinse the salmon clean.

Smoke whole fillets with the meat side up, in the smoker, until done. A full 3-5 pound fillet side will need about 2-3 hours at a smoking temperature of 200°.

Approximate Cooking Time: 2-3 hours

Wood Suggestion: Fruit wood- Apple or Cherry

HONEY MARINATED LOBSTER TAILS

Use only cold water tails when smoking lobster tails for a higher quality and sweeter product.

4 each	Lobster Tails, out of shell
1 batch	Honey Marinade for Lobster Tails (pg. 133)

After removing the tail meat from the shells (save shells to make shellfish stock) turn the tails over and using a sharp knife put 3-4 small slits across the width of the tails about 1" apart. This will help keep the tails from curling up when cooking. Place the tail meat in a pan or glass dish and pour marinade over the tails. Marinade two hours. After marinating, drain tails well, get smoker to 200° and place the tails in the smoker. Smoke until flesh is just set or internal temperature of 155°.

Approximate Cooking Time: 1- 1 1/2 hours

Wood Suggestion: Maple

COCONUT CURRIED SCALLOPS

This makes beautiful gold nuggets of sweetness. The combination of coconut and curry make for an outstanding flavor.

1 pound	Scallops, 1" in diameter
1 batch	Coconut Curry Marinade (pg. 134)

Remove the side muscle from the scallop before marinating, pour marinade over the scallops and marinade for 2 hours.

After marinating, drain scallops well, get smoker to 200° and place the scallops in the smoker.

Approximate Cooking Time: 30 - 45 minutes

Wood Suggestion: Maple

MUSTARD MARINATED SHRIMP

Do not over marinate the shrimp, this will cause the shrimp to be tough and over cook.

1 pound	Shrimp, peeled & cleaned 16/20 ct.
1 cup	Mustard Marinade (pg. 134)

Peel and clean the shrimp, place the shrimp in a glass bowl or dish. Pour the marinade over the shrimp and toss to coat evenly. Allow the shrimp to marinade about 30 minutes. Over-marinating the shrimp will cause them to be tough.

After marinating, drain shrimp well, get smoker to 200° and place the shrimps in the smoker.

Approximate Cooking Time: 30 - 45 minutes

Wood Suggestion: Maple

BBQ SPICED CATFISH

I like adding some lemon pepper to the brine when doing catfish.

10 each	Catfish Fillets, skinned
1 batch	Smoked Trout Brine (page 109), cold
2 TB.	Lemon Pepper
as needed	Backyard Chicken Rub (pg. 118)

Place the catfish fillets into the brine with the lemon pepper. Marinate in the brine for 8 hours only.

After marinating, remove from the brine and pat dry with a clean cloth or towel. Air dry the fillets for one hour under refrigeration. And place catfish fillets on the racks in the smoker skin-side down. Sprinkle the top side of the fillets lightly with the Backyard Chicken Rub. Smoke at 200°. Smoke until just done.

Notes: The chicken rub lends itself well to the lighter white fish, because of the herbal poultry seasoning in the rub.

Try using different seasonings for added flavor. Add the seasoning after you have place the fillets on your smoker rack.

Approximate Cooking Time: 45-60 minutes

Wood Suggestion: Oak or Maple

HONEY MAPLE SALMON

The sweetness of this brine matches well with the moist texture of the salmon fillets.

2 each	3 lbs. Salmon Fillets, boned, skinless
1 batch	Honey Maple Salmon Brine (page 110), cold

Place the boneless fillets with the skin side down into a shallow pan or dish. Pour the brine over the salmon fillets and marinate in the brine for 8 hours only.

After marinating, remove from the brine and pat dry with a clean cloth or towel. Air dry the fillets for one hour under refrigeration. Place on the racks in the smoker skin side down at 200°. Smoke until just done.

Approximate Cooking Time: 2 hours minutes

Wood Suggestion: Maple

Mops

"Hell" Fire Brisket Mop
"Spicy" Maple Rib Mop
Apple Cider Rib Mop
Backyard BBQ Mop
Cherry Rib Mop
Mustard Mop for Spareribs
H & M Brisket Mop
"Take My Breath Away" Rib Mop
Honey Brown Sugar Rib Mop
Margarita Mop For Chicken
Nawlins' Butter Mop
Pulled Pork Mop
Basic Rib Mop
Sweet & Sour Mop
Dr. Pepper® Rib Mop
Spiced Brisket Mop
Whiskey Brisket Mop

"HELL" FIRE BRISKET MOP

This mop will kick up the "heat" flavor of your brisket!

1 1/2 cups	Rice Wine Vinegar
1 cup	Beef Broth, canned
1/2 cup	Asian Chili Paste
1/2 cup	Sugar, superfine
1/2 cup	Soy Sauce
1/4 cup	Molasses
1/4 cup	Worcestershire Sauce
4 TB.	Yellow Mustard
1 1/2 TB.	Rub Me Tender™ Rub (page 113)
1/4 cup	Olive Oil

Combine all ingredients together in a stainless steel bowl, except for the olive oil. Mix and blend well. Whisk the olive oil into the mixture and hold at room temperature for service.

Notes: You can adjust the 'heat of this Mop, by increasing or decreasing the Asian Chili Paste.

Enough for one brisket.

"SPICY" MAPLE RIB MOP

Nice combination of flavors with the maple syrup and pick a pepper sauce.

1 cup	Water
1 cup	Pineapple Juice, canned
1 cup	Maple Syrup, "real"
2 TB.	Margarine, melted
1/4 cup	White Vinegar
4 TB.	Worcestershire sauce
4 TB.	A-1® Steak Sauce
3 TB.	Pick a Pepper Sauce, brown
1 tsp.	Chili Powder
1 tsp.	Hot Sauce, red

Combine all the ingredients together and blend well. Place on the heat and bring to a boil. Remove as soon as the mop begins to boil.

Allow to stand overnight to blend flavors. Keep warm during the basting process.

Notes: This Mop is GREAT on spare ribs and pork tenderloins.

Enough for 6 pounds of meat.

APPLE CIDER RIB MOP

I like using cider when making mops, the sorghum adds a nice color to the mop and ribs.

1 cup	Brown Sugar
1 1/2 quarts	Apple Cider, fresh
3/4 cup	White Vinegar, distilled
1 cup	Maple syrup, "real"
1/2 cup	Sorghum
2 TB.	Asian Chili Paste

Combine the ingredients together and blend well to dissolve the brown sugar completely. Place the mop in a spray bottle and set on misting spray. Use with ribs after one hour of smoking. Spray sop ribs every 1 hour.

Heat flavor can be adjusted by increasing or decreasing the chili paste

Enough for 6 slabs of ribs.

BACKYARD BBQ MOP

This is one of my original mops used to win our Grand Champion Award at the American Royal.

12 ounces	Margarine, melted
1/2 cup	White Vinegar
2 tsp.	Worcestershire sauce
2 tsp.	A-1® Steak Sauce
1 tsp.	Hot Sauce
1 TB.	Lemon Pepper
3/4 cup	Barbecue Sauce, your favorite

Melt the margarine, and remove from the heat. Add the remaining ingredients, stir to blend well.

Enough for 3 slabs of ribs

CHERRY RIB MOP

I like the use of concentrate here, mix with the apple cider.

1 cup	Brown Sugar
1 1/2 quarts	Cherry Juice, made from concentrate
1/2 quart	Apple Cider, fresh
3/4 cup	White Vinegar, distilled
1/2 cup	Sorghum
3 TB.	Asian Chili Paste

Combine the ingredients together and blend well to dissolve the brown sugar completely.

Heat flavor can be adjusted by increasing or decreasing the Chili Paste

Enough for 8 slabs of ribs.

MUSTARD MOP FOR SPARERIBS

This is a good, standard mustard mop.

1/3 cup	Brown Sugar, light
1/4 cup	White Vinegar
1/4 cup	Pineapple Juice
1/4 cup	Mustard, yellow pourable

Combine the ingredients together and blend well to dissolve the brown sugar completely.

I like to bring this one to a quick boil to dissolve the mustard and sugar completely.

Enough for 2 slabs of ribs.

H & M BRISKET MOP

This mop combines the heat of horseradish with mustard for a great flavor.

1 1/2 cups	White Vinegar
1 cup	Teriyaki Sauce
1 cup	Horseradish
1/2	Stone Ground Mustard
1/4 cup	Rice Wine Vinegar
1/4 cup	Molasses
1/4 cup	Worcestershire Sauce
1 1/2 TB.	Rub Me Tender™ Rub (page 113)
1/2 cup	Olive Oil

Combine all ingredients together in a stainless steel bowl, except for the olive oil. Mix and blend well. Whisk the oil into the mixture and hold at room temperature for service.

Notes: Enough to mop two brisket flats.

"TAKE MY BREATH AWAY" RIB MOP

Breathe some life into your ribs with this mop!

2 cups	Pineapple Nectar or Juice
1 each	Pick A Pepper Sauce, brown (5 oz. Bottles)
1/4 cup	Worcestershire Sauce
1/4	A-1® Steak Sauce
1/2 cup	Maple Syrup, "real"

Combine all ingredients together and place on the heat. Bring to a boil and remove from the heat, hold warm for use.

HONEY BROWN SUGAR RIB MOP

One of several mops, that require the use of Dr, Pepper®.

1 can	Dr. Pepper®, warm
1/2 cup	White Vinegar, distilled
1/2 cup	Honey
1/2 cup	Sorghum
1/4 cup	Maple Syrup, "real"
1/4 cup	Brown Sugar
1 TB.	Asian Chili Paste

Combine all ingredients together and bring to a quick boil to dissolve the sugars. Remove from the heat and allow to cool down.

Hold warm for use.

Notes: If refrigerating, bring back to a warm temperature before using to insure the sugars stay incorporated in the Mop.

MARGARITA MOP FOR CHICKEN

A simple mop with lots of flavor!

1/4 cup	Honey
1/4 cup	Triple Sec
1/4 cup	Lime Juice, "real"
1/4 cup	Tequila

Mix all the ingredients together and blend well. Store in a container until needed.

Enough for 3 pounds of chicken.

NAWLINS' BUTTER MOP

Use for a baste or marinade.
Great on poultry and seafood! Outstanding on turkey!

12 ounces	Margarine
3/4 cup	Garlic, minced
2 tsp.	Black Pepper, fine grind
2 tsp.	Crushed Red Pepper, flakes
2 tsp.	Crab Boil
3 TB.	Paprika
4 ounces	Brown Sugar
2 tsp.	Garlic Salt
3 TB.	Pick a Pepper Sauce, brown
2 ounces	A-1® Steak Sauce
2 ounces	Worcestershire Sauce
5 cups	Water
1 each	Lemon, halved

Melt butter and margarine in heavy kettle. Place the chopped garlic and all dry spices in cheesecloth and tie. Add the bag of spices along with brown sugar to the melted butter mixture. Let saute for about 10 minutes. Add bottle sauces then water and lemons. Slowly bring to a boil. Take off heat and reserve until service.

PULLED PORK MOP

One of the secrets to my award winning pork!

1 cup	"Take Your Breath Away" BBQ Sauce (pg. 97)
1 cup	White Vinegar
4 TB.	Hot Sauce
2 TB.	Pulled Pork Rub (page 117)
4 TB.	Pick a Pepper Sauce, brown

Combine all ingredients, blending well. Heat slowly to a slight simmer, DO NOT BOIL!

Hold warm for service.

Notes: Enough for 1 large or two small pork butts.

BASIC RIB MOP

This mop works well, cause it keeps the ribs sweet and moist. Lends itself well to all finishing sauces or flavors.

2 cups	Pineapple Juice, canned
1 cup	Water
1/2 cup	White Vinegar

Combine all ingredients together. Hold for service.

Enough for 4 slabs of ribs.

SWEET & SOUR MOP

Use on Spareribs, Baby Back Ribs, Country Spareribs or Pork Butts, gives a nice oriental flavor.

1 cup	Rice Wine Vinegar
1/2 cup	Honey
1/2 cup	Salad Oil
1/4 cup	Brown Sugar
1/4 cup	Soy Sauce, lite
1 tsp.	Crushed Red Pepper Flakes

Combine all the ingredients together and stir well. Reserve for mopping of ribs.

DR. PEPPER® RIB MOP

Another good mop using Dr. Pepper® to add a new demension to your mopping liquid.

8 ounces	Dr. Pepper®
3 ounces	Pineapple Nectar or Juice
2 ounces	Water
1 ounce	White Vinegar
3 TB.	Brown Sugar

Combine all ingredients together. Hold for service.

Enough for 2 slabs of ribs.

SPICED BRISKET MOP

Once cooled down, this makes for a great brisket marinade also. Excellent mop for doing whole briskets or flats.

3 cup	Beef Stock
3/4 cup	Worcestershire Sauce
1/2 cup	Tomato Catsup
1/2 cup	Lemon Juice, fresh
2 TB.	Yellow Mustard
1 TB.	Asian Chili Paste
1 TB.	Chili Powder
1 tsp.	Celery Seed, ground
2 tsp.	Seasoning Salt
1 tsp.	Cumin, ground
1 tsp.	Granulated Onion

Combine the ingredients together in a nonreactive pot and bring to a boil. Simmer for 10 minutes remove from the heat and cool slightly.

When using as a mop keep warm.

Heat flavor can be adjusted by increasing or decreasing the chili paste

Enough for one 6-8 pound flat.

WHISKEY BRISKET MOP

Nice flavor combination with the whiskey and pineapple juice.

1 cup	Water
1 cup	Pineapple Juice, canned
1/2 cup	Whiskey
1/4 cup	White Vinegar
2 TB.	Margarine
2 1/2 tsp.	Black Pepper, table grind
1 TB.	Chili Powder
2 tsp.	Kosher Salt
3 TB.	Worcestershire Sauce
1 tsp.	Onion Powder
1 tsp.	Dry Mustard
1 tsp.	Hot Sauce
1 tsp.	Garlic Powder

Combine all the ingredients in a sauce pot and bring to a boil. Remove from the heat and allow to stand overnight to blend flavors.

Keep warm during the mopping process.

Enough for one brisket.

Salsa & Relishes

Balsamic Tomatoes
Chunky Fresh Salsa
Cucumber Salsa
Gazpacho Salsa
Melon-Cilantro Relish
Papaya-Pineapple Relish
Pineapple Salsa
Red & Yellow Tomato Relish
Tomato-Green Olive Relish
Warm Jalapeno Corn Relish

BALSAMIC TOMATOES

Excellent in the summer. Made with home grown tomatoes!

4 pounds	Tomatoes, peeled & seeded, medium dice
2 TB.	Roasted Garlic, minced
1/2 cup	Balsamic vinegar
1/2 cup	Olive oil
1 1/2 ounces	Basil, julienned
1 tsp.	Kosher Salt
1 tsp.	Black Pepper, coarse grind

After preparing the tomatoes, place them in a stainless steel bowl. Add the minced garlic. Season the tomato and garlic mixture. Mix the vinegar and olive together, whisking slightly to blend. Pour over the tomatoes and let sit for 3 hours at least before serving.

Notes: Tomatoes are best served and eaten at room temperature!

Great Starter Dish!

Enough for 10-12 people.

CHUNKY FRESH SALSA

Make lots of this recipe in the summer with home grown tomatoes, makes a good canning salsa for the winter.

*** SALSA BASE ***

1-28 oz. can	Crushed Tomatoes, in heavy puree
1/2 tsp.	Kosher Salt
2 tsp.	Worcestershire Sauce
1/2 tsp.	Garlic Powder
1/2 tsp.	Cumin, ground

*** FRESH BASE ***

3 cup	Tomatoes, fresh, small diced
3/4 cups	White Onions, small diced
4 TB.	Jalapeno Peppers, minced
4 TB.	Cilantro, fresh, minced

*** OPTIONAL ***

2 TB.	Chiles, peeled, seeds removed, roasted

Place the salsa-based products in a clean container and blend to mix. Add the fresh base, after it is prepared, to the salsa base and stir to blend ingredients well. Let the salsa sit in refrigerator for at least 4 hours, adjust flavors and thickness if needed.

Makes about 2 quarts.

CUCUMBER SALSA

Excellent with chicken dishes.

8 each	Cucumber, peeled and seeded, 1/2" diced
1 medium	Red Onion, 1/4" dice
1 medium	Green Pepper, 1/4" dice
1 bunch	Green Onions, minced
1 each	Jalapeno, seeded and minced
12 each	Roma Tomatoes, seeded and chopped, 1/2"
1 bunch	Cilantro, minced
1/2 cup	White Vinegar
1/4 cup	Salad Oil
to taste	Salt and pepper

Peel and seed the cucumbers. Medium dice the cucumbers and place them in a bowl. Clean and seed all the peppers including the jalapenos. Chop the peppers and tomatoes, add them to the diced cucumbers. Add the cilantro, mix gently. Combine the vinegar and oil, pour over the mixture. Season with salt and pepper. Let sit for 4 hours before using in the refrigerator.

Notes: Best when made 4 hours ahead of time.

Enough for 8-10 people.

GAZPACHO SALSA

Save this one for smoked shellfish!

12 each	Cucumber, peeled, chopped 1/2"
4 each	Tomatoes, peeled, seeded and chopped, 1/2"
1 each	Red Onion, small diced, 1/4"
1 each	Red Pepper, small diced, 1/4"
1 each	Yellow Pepper, small diced, 1/4"
1 each	Green Pepper, small diced, 1/4"
1 1/2 bunches	Cilantro, minced
1/2 cup	White Wine Vinegar
1/2 cup	Olive Oil
to taste	Salt and Pepper
1/8 cup	Garlic, minced

Clean and diced the peppers and green onions. Peel and seed the cucumbers and dice the same size as the peppers and onions. Add the cilantro, vinegar, oil, garlic and seasonings to the mixture and mix well. Refrigerate until needed or ready to serve.

Notes: Best when made 4 hours in advance.

Enough for 12-15 people.

MELON - CILANTRO RELISH

Outstanding with Pork dishes!

1 each	Honey Dew Melon, peeled and chopped, 1/2"
2 each	Cantaloupe, peeled, chopped, 1/2"
1 small	Red Pepper, small diced, 1/4"
1 small	Red Onion, small diced, 1/4"
1 bunch	Cilantro, minced
1/4 cup	Honey
1/8 cup	Rice Wine Vinegar
2 1/2 TB.	Vegetable Salt
1/4 cup	Salad Oil
3 TB.	Tabasco Sauce, green
1 tsp.	Black Pepper, cracked

Dice all the melons into a medium dice, fine dice the red peppers and onion. Clean and mince the cilantro. Mix well the vinegar, oil and seasoning. Place all the ingredients in a bowl and toss with the seasoned vinegar and oil.

Notes: Make sure to use ripened melons for a full flavor.
Best to let melon sit out for a day before making relish.

Enough for 15 people.

PAPAYA-PINEAPPLE RELISH

Good with smoked porkloin or pork tenderloin.

1 each	Pineappl, peeled & diced, 1/2"
2 each	Papaya, peeled & diced. 1/2"
1 cup	Red and Green Bell Peppers, seeded & small dice, 1/4" (50/50)
1/2 cup	Salad Oil
1 TB.	Sesame Seed Oil
1/4 cup	Cider Vinegar
to taste	Salt and Pepper

Combine the pineapple, papayas & red pepper in a stainless steel bowl & toss. Add the remainder of the ingredient & toss.

Notes: Make sure the papaya is fully ripe before making relish.

Enough for 10 people.

PINEAPPLE SALSA

Great with smoked shellfish and whitefish,
I like it with smoked catfish fillets. too!

1 each	Pineapple, peeled, cored, sliced
1 each	Red Bell Pepper, 1/2 inch diced
1 each	Green Bell Pepper, 1/2 inch diced
1 each	Red Onion, chopped fine, 1/4"
1/4 cup	Salad Oil
3 TB.	Cilantro, minced
2 TB.	Lime Juice, fresh
2 TB.	Chives, minced
2 TB.	Parsley, minced
1 each	Serrano Pepper, minced

After preparing the pineapple, peppers and jalapeons, grill them over medium heat until the pineapples are slightly caramelized and the peppers are slightly charred. Rough chop the pineapple. Dice the peppers and add to the chopped pineapple. Mix with the onion, oil, cilantro, lime juice, chives, parsley and chiles. Serve the salsa warm or room temperature.

Enough for 12-15 people.

RED & YELLOW TOMATO RELISH

Outstanding with smoked turkey dishes.

1 pound	Vine Ripe Tomatoes , diced 1/2"
1/2 pound	Yellow Tomatoes, diced 1/2"
1/2 pound	Green Apples , diced 1/2"
1 medium	Red Onion, diced 1/4"
2 cloves	Garlic, minced
1 cup	Red Wine Vinegar
1/2 tsp.	Allspice, ground
1 tsp.	Cinnamon, ground
1 tsp.	Ginger, ground
1/2 tsp.	Red Pepper Flakes
1 1/2 cups	Brown Sugar, light
to taste	Salt and pepper
1 TB.	Oil

Saute the onions and garlic lightly in the oil. Add the rest of the ingredients, except for the brown sugar. Cook for 10 to 15 minutes. Remove from the heat and add the brown sugar, stirring in well. Cool down and refrigerate.

Notes: Best when made 24 hours in advance.

Enough for 10 people.

TOMATO-GREEN OLIVE RELISH

This relish is great with Smoked Porkloin or a darker colored fish, like Bluefish, Tuna or Mackerel.

8 ounces	Green Olives, small dice
8 ounces	Plum Tomatoes, seeded & small dice, 1/4"
4 ounces	Shallots, minced
1 TB.	Garlic, minced
2 TB.	Fresh Oregano, chopped
2 TB.	Fresh Parsley, chopped
1/4 cup	Balsamic Vinegar
1/2 cup	Olive Oil
1 TB.	Black Pepper, coarse ground
1 TB.	Kosher Salt

Combine all of the ingredient except the oil & vinegar in a stainless steel bowl. Combine the oil & vinegar and whisk to form a vinaigrette. Stir the oil & vinegar into the olive mixture & hold the relish for service.

Enough for 6 people.

WARM JALAPENO CORN RELISH

The is a great accompaniment for Smoked Salmon!

2 pounds	Corn Kernels, frozen
4 each	Roma Tomato medium dice
1/2 cups	Red and Green Bell Peppers, medium dice, 1/2"
2 each	Jalapeno, thinly sliced rounds
1/4 cup	Onion, medium dice, 1/2"
1 TB.	Garlic, chopped
2 tsp.	Black Pepper, ground
1 TB.	Kosher Salt
2 tsp.	Chili Powder
1 TB.	Butter, melted

In butter, saute onions and peppers until onions are translucent. Add remaining ingredients. Cook for fifteen minutes and cool. Salt and pepper to taste.

Notes: Hold warm for serving or cool down and reheat when needed.

Enough for 6-8 people.

Side Dishes

"Zesty" Backyard Baked Beans
Boston Baked Beans
Creamy Cole Slaw
Dill Potato Salad
Foil Roasted Potatoes
Jambalaya Rice
Health Salad
Pea & Cheese Salad
Smoked Bacon & Onion Baked Beans
Wisconsin Cheddar Potato Salad
Smoked Gorgonzola Mushrooms

"ZESTY" BACKYARD BAKED BEANS

The longer the beans are in your smoker the better they are. Allow them to slow cook under your smoking meats for added flavor!

1/2 pound	Smoked Meat Scrapes, small diced
1/2 pound	White Onions, finely chopped
6 ounces	Tomato Paste
1/3 cup	Brown Sugar
1/4 cup	Molasses
1/4 cup	Sorghum Syrup
1 TB.	Dry Mustard
1/4 cup	White Vinegar
1/2 cup	Water
1 TB.	"Rub Me Tender™" Rub (page 113)
1 1/2 TB.	Chili Powder
1 TB.	Liquid Smoke flavoring
1 ea.	"BUSH"® Beans in Tomato Sauce Country Style BBQ (27 oz. can)
1-16 oz. can	"BUSH"® Pinto Beans, canned, rinsed
1-16 oz. can	"BUSH"® Great Northern Beans, canned, rinsed
1/4 cup	Brown Sugar

Place all the ingredients into a heavy baking pan, stirring well to blend all the ingredients evenly. Top the beans with the additional brown sugar. Place the beans in the smoker and allow to cook along with the meats.

Beans can take a tremendous amount of smoke flavor. This will only enhance the flavor of the beans.

Enough for 10-15 people.

Approximate Cooking Time: 2-3 hours

BOSTON BAKED BEANS

These beans are worth the long cooking process. This is a very old recipe from my many travels to Boston.

1/2 cup	Molasses
1/4 cup	Brown Sugar
1 TB.	Kosher Salt
1 TB.	Dry Mustard
1 tsp.	All Spice, ground
1/2 tsp.	Cayenne, ground
2 cups	Ham Stock
4 pounds	Northern Beans, dry
6 ounces	White Onions, thinly sliced
1/2 pound	Salt Pork, cubed

Wash and soak the dry beans over night. Picking through them and discarding the bad ones.

Mix the molasses, brown sugar, salt and spices together to form a paste. Brown the salt pork until crisp. Add the drained soaked beans, sliced onions and the molasses mixture. Then add the ham stock, bring to a boil.

Put into a roasting pan or heavy skillet, cover tightly with foil. Place on the top of the fire box and bring to a boil. Bake in smoker at 250° for 4 hours. Remove the cover and smoke for about another hour. Add more stock if the beans seem dry.

Enough for 12-15 people.

Approximate Cooking Time: 5-6 hours

CREAMY COLE SLAW

This makes an awesome cole slaw. Make a lot because they will eat it all. I prefer cream cole slaws over the vinegar style.

3 pounds	White Cabbage, shredded
3/4 cup	Carrots, shredded
3 cups	Mayonnaise, heavy
1 cup	Sour Cream
1/2 cup	Sugar, granulated
1 small	White Onion, minced
1 TB.	Yellow Mustard, pourable
1 ounce	White Vinegar, distilled

Clean and shred, the cabbage and carrots, and mix together. Make the dressing by adding the mayonnaise, sour cream, sugar, vinegar, onions and mustard together and blend well. Combine the dressing with the cabbage/carrot mixture. Mix well.

Let the cole slaw set in the refrigerator for 4 hours before serving.

Notes: Extra flavors can be a nice addition to this recipe (i.e. green peppers, scallions, chives).

Enough for 15-20 people.

DILL POTATO SALAD

Salad flavor is better when the salad is made a day ahead!

3 pounds	Baby Red Potatoes, large diced, cooked
1 cup	Celery, diced
1/2 cup	Green Onions, diced
1 cup	Sour Cream
1 cup	Mayonnaise
1 ounce	Dijon Mustard
1/8 cup	White Vinegar
3 TB.	Fresh Dill, minced
to taste	Kosher Salt
to taste	White Pepper

Dice and cook the potatoes the day before, cook until almost done, drain and chill well before making salad.

Combine the remaining ingredients with the potatoes, blending well. Cover and refrigerate until needed.

Enough for 10 people.

FOIL ROASTED POTATOES

Great replacement for the old bake potato!

6 large	Russet Potatoes, washed
1 medium	White Onion, sliced thin
1/4 cup	Olive Oil
1/4 stick	Butter, sliced
1 TB.	Kosher Salt
1 TB.	Black Pepper
1 tsp.	Chili Powder
1 tsp.	Paprika

Slice the potatoes and place in a stainless steel bowl. Add the sliced onions, sprinkle the potatoes and onions with the oil and dry seasonings. Toss well. Place the mixture on aluminum foil. Slice the butter on top of the mixture and fold the foil to form a sealed bag.

Place potatoes in the hottest area of your smoker. Cook until potatoes are tender.

Notes: Foil roasting bags work get for these potatoes.

Enough for 6-8 people.

JAMBALAYA RICE

This will be a huge hit with your friends.
Stir the rice well just before serving.

1 1/2 cups	Rice, uncooked, medium grain
1 pounds	Smoked Sausage, sliced 1/4" thick
1 pound	Chicken Breast, medium dice
1/2 pound	Shrimp, med. size, peeled, cleaned
1/2 pound	Ham, medium dice
3 ounces	White Onions, medium dice
3 ounces	Celery, medium dice
1/2 each	Green Bell Pepper, medium dice
1/2 cup	Green Onion, sliced thin
2 TB.	Chicken Base
3/4 cup	Tomato Puree
1 1/2 TB.	Season Salt
1 TB.	Sweet Basil, dry
1 TB.	Oregano, dry
1 each	Bay leaf
1 TB.	Thyme Leaves, dry
1 TB.	Garlic Salt
2 TB.	Sugar
2 TB.	Worcestershire Sauce
1 tsp.	Cayenne Pepper, ground
3 cups	Water, warmed

Place the rice in a 4" deep half pan. Add to the rice, the meats, vegetables, base, seasonings, tomato puree and water. Stir the jambalaya mixture together well to mix in all ingredients and spices.

Place the pan on top of the fire box, and bring rice to a boil. Once boiling, place the pan of jambalaya into the smoker below your smoking meats. Cook until rice is swelled and the moisture is absorbed and the meats are cooked.

Enough for 10-12 people.

HEALTH SALAD

Best to make this salad about an hour before serving and serve at room temperature for a fuller flavor.

3 medium	Tomatoes, vine ripened, large diced, 1 1/2"
1 large	Cucumbers, peeled, seeded, 1/2"
1 small	White Onions, thinly sliced
4 each	Scallions, bias sliced, thin
1/4 cup	Olive Oil
1/2 cup	Balsamic Vinegar
2 tsp.	Kosher Salt
2 tsp.	Black Pepper, table grind

After preparing the cucumbers (dicing large) and tomatoes, place them into a glass bowl. Add the sliced onions and scallions. Drizzle the mixture, add the vinegar and seasonings. Toss the salad gently to mix well. Cover and let sit for 2-3 hours before serving.

Notes: This salad can also be made white distilled vinegar. An assortment of fresh herbs lends itself well to the flavors of the salad (i.e. basil, oregano, thyme).

Enough for 6 people.

PEA & CHEESE SALAD

This salad is best made the night before.
Great change for the summer barbecue.

1 pounds	Green Peas, frozen
3 ounces	American Cheese, unsliced, small diced, 1/4"
1/2 cup	Scallions, sliced thin
1 each	Hard Cooked Eggs, medium dice
1 ounce	Sun-Dried Tomatoes, small diced
3/4 cups	Miracle Whip®
1/4 cup	Sour Cream, fresh
1 TB.	White Vinegar, distilled
1 TB.	Sugar, granulated
1 pinch	Kosher Salt
1 pinch	White Pepper

Do not cook or blanch the peas in any way, use them frozen. Break the frozen peas apart and toss with the cheese, scallions, eggs and tomatoes distributing well. Mix the Miracle Whip, sour cream, vinegar, sugar and seasonings together using a wire whip. Pour over the pea mixture and mix thoroughly.

This Salad needs to be refrigerated for 12 hours before serving.

Enough for 4-6 people.

SMOKED BACON & ONION BAKED BEANS

They have a very nice flavor from the caramelizing of the onions and bacon.

1/2 pound	Raw Bacon, med. diced
1/2 pound	White Onions, finely chopped
1/2 cup	Brown Sugar
1/4 cup	Molasses
1/4 cup	Sorghum Syrup
4 TB.	Yellow Mustard, pourable
1-27 oz. can	"BUSH"® Country Style Beans
1-16 oz. can	"BUSH"® Pinto Beans, canned, rinsed
1-16 oz. can	"BUSH"® Great Northern Beans, canned rinsed
1/2 cup	"Take Away My" BBQ Sauce (page 97)
1 tsp.	"Rub Me Tender™" Rub (page 113)

Place the diced bacon in a heavy roaster pan or skillet. Place on the firebox lid or over the fire grate of the smoker. Once crisp and rendered add the onions. Cook until transparent and soft then add the sugar to dissolve. Cook until the mixture starts to caramelize and thicken.

Once the mixture is caramelized remove from the heat. Add the Country Style Beans and the drained beans to the mixture. Add remaining ingredients and stir to blend well.

Place in the smoker below any smoking meats. This will add additional flavor to your beans.

Notes: Make sure to stir, while caramelizing the bacon and onion mixture. Do not allow to burn!!

Enough for 10-15 people.

Approximate Cooking Time: 2-3 hours

WISCONSIN CHEDDAR POTATO SALAD

This is a very old family recipe from my early years living in America's Dairyland!

5 pounds	Red Skinned Potatoes, 3/4" dice
8 ounces	Cheddar Cheese, shredded
3 each	Hard Cooked Eggs, chopped
2 ounces	White Onions, finely chopped
4 TB.	Fresh Chives, minced
2 TB.	Salad Sprinkle, "McCormick's"®
1 tsp.	White Pepper, ground
2 tsp.	Season Salt
3 TB.	Pourable Mustard, "French's"®
3 cups	Mayonnaise, "Hellmann's"®

Cook the potatoes till just done, cool immediately. Put the potatoes into a large stainless bowl, combine all the ingredients with the cooled potatoes. Mix well, stirring to combine the salad very well. Cover and chill for at least 4 hours before serving.

Red skinned potatoes work the best for this salad, cause they hold up better to the cooking process. You want to have a firmer textured potato for your salad. Salad can also be made with Gold Yukon potatoes.

Enough for 15-20 people.

SMOKED GORGONZOLA MUSHROOMS with Sun-dried Tomato Pesto

These are the Famous Rib Stars® Mushrooms!

12 each	Crimni Mushrooms, washed & clean
1/4 cup	Sun-dried Tomato Pesto, prepared
4 ounces	Gorgonzola Cheese, crumbled

After removing the stems and washing the mushrooms, turn them with the cavity side down on some paper towels, to absorb the excess moisture. When dry, fill the cavity of the mushroom cap with 1 tsp. of the Sun-dried Tomato Pesto. Top with a small amount of Gorgonzola cheese.

Place in a 200° smoker and smoke for about 15 minutes. Just until cheese starts to melt and filling is warm. To long of a cooking period will make the mushrooms soft and hard to handle. Serve immediately.

Serves 4 -6 people.

SUN-DRIED TOMATO PESTO

1 Jar	Sun-dried Tomatoes, in oil, 24 ounce
1/2 cup	Garlic, fresh, peeled
1 cup	Walnuts
1/3 cup	Sage, fresh, chopped
8 ounces	Parmesan Cheese, grated
1 cup	Olive Oil
to taste	Salt & Pepper

Place everything in a food processor except the Olive oil, salt, pepper and parmesan cheese. When finely chopped in the cuisinart, mix in the remaining ingredients.

Hold in refrigerator for use or freeze leftover product.

Makes about 1 quart.

Index

DEF

GH

IJKL

MNO

PQ

R

S

TUV

WXYZ

BACKYARD BBQ NOTES

BACKYARD BBQ NOTES

BACKYARD BBQ NOTES

BACKYARD BBQ NOTES